Safety, Security, and Peace of Mind

Safety, Security, and Peace of Mind

Keeping People Safe Where They Live

Salvatore DeRose, Sr.

Safety, Security, and Peace of Mind

Keeping People Safe Where They Live

For more information, please contact the author directly at: sderose@Signal88.com

ISBN: 978-0-9983596-0-1

Editorial services provided by: Stephanie J. Beavers Communications
Cover design provided by: Rashmita Paul
Interior artwork provided by: Biddle Design

Dedication

To my beautiful grandchildren who always make me smile
and hope for a safer tomorrow.

Make all your wildest dreams come true!

Love, *Grumples*

CONTENTS

Introduction 1

Chapter 1: How Safe Are We? 7

Chapter 2: Residence Type and the Right Security Strategy .. 23

Chapter 3: Apartments 33

Chapter 4: Townhome Communities and Condominiums 45

Chapter 5: Age-Restricted Communities 53

Chapter 6: Dormitories, Residence Halls, Student Housing ... 61

Chapter 7: Mixed-Use Properties 71

Chapter 8: Why Hire a Professional Security Company?........ 75

Chapter 9: Why Signal 88 Security?....................................... 85

Chapter 10: A Day in the Life of Signal 88 Security Heroes .. 105

Appendix 111

FOREWORD

Our *peace of mind* experiences disruptions every day. When we turn on the news, check our favorite internet portals, review email, socialize with friends, drive down the street, or spend time in our communities, an ever-present level of concern keeps us on edge.

As I did my first thorough look into the security industry nearly a decade ago, I realized it is an industry based fundamentally on trust. As communities, access to information, and assets and liabilities continue to grow and spread, so will the need for security and the need for the security industry. The threats to peace of mind originate and expand as those with criminal intent have increased access to information and technology, which they will use to disrupt peace of mind throughout the communities where people live, work, and congregate.

The establishments that address security issues are presumptively the police—on a local or regional level—and the military—on a global stage. As statistics throughout this book show, crime continues to increase and, as research methods improve with technology, more time and money are required to address these concerns. This phenomenon further expands the gap between crime and the ability to address crime with policing, and leaves the police in more and more of a position to provide only a reactive response to this ever-increasing need. The gap between crime and our ability to address it is clearly widening.

Professional security services and companies, therefore, are intended to fill the gap left in the wake of increased crime with diminished resources. Organizations such as those defined in this book employ private security services to mitigate the risks that are eloquently communicated by author Sal DeRose throughout the middle chapters. At the same time, as the world, access to information, and our culture change, security companies must likewise evolve to meet how the criminal approach to these changes impacts our ability to live in peace—and with peace of mind.

The Signal 88 Security concept was born with the intention of maintaining people's and communities' peace of mind. To fill the increased-crime-with-diminished-resources gap, people such as Sal, who carry a passion and long-term commitment to their community, step in and take on franchise ownership. As members of a franchise network, owners are unified in training and information, unlike the segregated nature of police departments, and able to build upon the outstanding training and experience of previous careers to go into business for themselves with the express purpose and design of closing the gap between crime and the place where people feel peace of mind.

The patrol model Sal speaks to also addresses the increased costs the industry faces by dividing the company's time and expense privately among multiple properties and clients, in the same manner in which public tax dollars in aggregate provide funding for a local police department. Additionally, the branding elements of a well-designed security company can enhance the deterrent effect, just as a police car parked on a roadway's median during morning commute serves to slow speeding vehicles down to the speed limit. Our security services are all powered by, and tracked with, innovative web-based technology to provide visibility and information previously unseen and unavailable in the security industry.

Throughout the book, Sal and his colleague franchisees do an excellent job of communicating the need for best-practice security and provide incredibly useful tips on how to both evaluate vulnerabilities and also to address the huge need for security for the safety of people, property, and possessions, wherever they reside.

I am honored to have Sal and many other franchisees like him join our organization with the passion to pursue serving our communities to create peace of mind within them, and in so doing, embrace and pursue their own passions in life! It is only by the collective efforts of our franchisees, our diligent officers, our organizational staff, and our many vendors that we are able to work together to accomplish this goal! As you read this book, I challenge you to think in what way you, too, can join us in this mission—whether as a client, officer, franchisee, or supporter—to create peace of mind in your community, your country, and our world.

Sincerely,

Reed Nyffeler
CEO, Signal 88 Security Franchise Group

Acknowledgements

I would like to thank my family for supporting me on this project and for putting up with my long days and nights.

I would also like to recognize and thank my fellow Signal 88 Security franchise owners whose support, anecdotes, quotes, advice, and other contributions added *depth* and *breadth* to this book - in particular, Zach Alsterberg, Jeff Carlyle, Jeff Chovan, Mike Daly, Toni Kosir, Pete Mango, and Kris Withrow.

A special thank you goes to Ed Leaman, of Growers and Nomads, for his insights into the world of branding and marketing, and to Stephanie Beavers of Stephanie J. Beavers Communications for her work on gathering and compiling the information necessary to tell the complete story of how property managers can keep residents safe.

And finally, I would like to thank Reed Nyffeler, CEO and cofounder of Signal 88 Security. His support and guidance on my Signal 88 journey has been invaluable. His courage of conscious leadership helps us all truly pursue our passions in life openly, freely, and joyfully.

Introduction

The search and yearning for peace of mind is universal and eternal. This book provides guidance and information on how people can find peace of mind vis-à-vis how safe and secure they feel where they live and play.

This book is intended for use primarily by property managers, landlords, homeowners' associations, and school officials for whom the safety of their tenants and residents matters. Throughout, the author shares valuable insights on how to keep residents safe in any type of multifamily residential environment, and provides tips *anyone* can follow to keep themselves and others safe. In addition, individual property and homeowners will also derive value from the material provided in this book, as much of the information can also be applied to single-family homeowners.

But don't be fooled. This book is not just a compilation of lists of what property managers and/or residents should or should not do to improve security in their communities. Readers will learn about the unique needs and challenges relating to security in a variety of residential types: apartments, townhomes and condominiums, college and university residence halls, age-restricted communities, and mixed-use buildings. In essence, this book is written to address the unique needs of a diverse group of communities and publics, and can be read from the perspective of either the resident/tenant or the property manager/landlord.

Security and safety are important and relevant needs for a broad swathe of people at different times and for different reasons.

Oftentimes, a professional security service is necessary so property managers, landlords, and homeowners/tenants are assured matters pertaining to security are handled correctly, legally, and thoroughly. Most private security companies have the expertise and knowledge to properly handle any type of security concern or threat.

Why Does Security Matter?

The United States Constitution contains no provision that guarantees the safety of people in their homes, schools, or places of business or recreation. But any fair-minded person would say they have a right to be and feel safe and secure in any environment, and take steps to ensure they are. In a multifamily residential community, the owner of that community has a legal responsibility to ensure the safety of the residents by protecting them against what is termed as reasonably foreseeable criminal conduct.

In fact, the law has proven over and over to be on the side of victims whose community management was deemed to be negligent by not providing an appropriately secure environment. Consider the following case, as presented in the article "Negligent Security; When Is Crime Your Problem?" by attorney Richards H. Ford. [1]

> In Garcia v. Wiener Wood Apartments, LLC, Miami-Dade County, Florida Circuit Court, 2008, Starsky Garcia was shot and killed by an unknown assailant in the parking lot of an apartment complex. The area in which the apartment was located had a history of violent or potentially violent crimes. The parameter [*sic*] fencing on the north and east side of the property was broken and had holes which allowed access from the adjacent properties. The fencing on the north side of the property had been damaged in the 2005 hurricane

---

[1] https://security.world/negligent-security-when-is-crime-your-problem/

season, and had never been repaired. The assault took place on December 8, 2006.

The estate claimed that although the complex was advertised as a gated community, the access control gate and exit gate had a long history of frequent malfunction and problems resulting from vandalism. The gates did not function properly for days at a time, allowing uncontrolled access to the property. At least one of the gates was broken and in the open position at the time of the homicide. The estate also argued that lighting conditions were unreasonably hazardous at the time of the murder. The estate claimed that the defendants failed to provide reasonable and adequate security on the premises and that the defendants failed to perform any type of periodic security audit of the property.

The estate argued that the defendants had failed to follow internal protocols for reporting incidents on the property, and that it failed to budget adequate resources to provide reasonable security measures on the property. The estate argued that the murder was foreseeable and preventable, and that but for the defendants' failure to correct known conditions, Mr. Garcia would not have been killed.

Testimony was elicited at trial from the defendants' leasing consultant, the regional manager, and the assistant regional manager, that information regarding the complexes' conditions was forwarded to the defendants' corporate officers in New York, and that the former employees had recommended repairing the fencing, lighting, and gating, as well as adding additional security patrols, but that all of the recommendations were denied by the defendants based upon budgetary concerns. The jury rendered a verdict in favor of the plaintiff *in the amount of $8,010,000.00.*

State laws and statutes vary, but property owners everywhere deal with similar issues that are potential concerns or legal liabilities in the event a victim makes a claim of negligent security: lighting on the premises and inside buildings; gates, fences, and other barriers; improper or lacking maintenance; unkempt landscaping; video surveillance; vandalism/trespassing/loitering; and their on-property security company. An ensuing investigation will attempt to establish that a property owner, manager, or landlord failed to maintain the residential property in proper condition or in compliance with codes, and this negligence led to the perpetration of a crime. As seen in the above example, the results were both deadly and costly.

Without a doubt, people who feel safe and secure in their home, no matter what type of home they live in, feel free to pursue their goals and their passions, and to live life to its fullest. People who do not feel safe relinquish independence and confidence. When forced to live in an unsafe, unsecure environment, some people experience mental health issues such as anxiety or depression. In fact, studies have shown a direct correlation between the lack of safety and the amount of stress—or distress—a person feels.[2]

The author of this book understands. He believes people and families want peace of mind—in their homes and schools, and in all commercial, retail, and institutional settings they frequent—and that these environments should afford residents, customers, and visitors the same peace of mind.

Property managers will learn insights and tips from law enforcement and security experts, and thus be able to take immediate short- and

---

[2] J. Booth, S. L. Ayers, F. F. Marsiglia, *Perceived Neighborhood Safety and Psychological Distress: Exploring Protective Factors.* https://www.wmich.edu/hhs/newsletters_journals/jssw_institutional/individual_subscribers/39.4.Booth.pdf

long-term steps to add to, or improve upon, security in the communities they manage.

The author would be remiss if a book on safety and security did not contain statistics, so you will find facts and data on certain crimes. The intent of this book is not to scare or alarm, but to provide an accurate portrait of crime levels in the United States and the good that is being done by heroes nationwide to combat it. And while the crime statistics pertain to only the U.S. market, the other information contained in the book has global and universal appeal.

Lastly, this book provides a look at one of the country's top private security companies, Signal 88 Security. Signal 88 Security understands and solves today's ever-increasing complex security needs, and they do so with simplicity, professionalism, value, and quality. To further reflect that sentiment, their employees are referred to as *officers*, not *guards*, though both words are used throughout the book in a general sense. Signal 88 Security, however, uses the word *officer* exclusively, to connote professionalism and convey an elevated sense of the services they provide, which ultimately gives those they protect an added sense of security.

With a tagline of "We're here," the company builds its trust on the peace of mind they provide their clients. Signal 88 Security is equally committed to helping individuals pursue their passions in life, and do so openly, freely, and joyfully. It is this author's commitment as well.

Chapter 1: How Safe Are We?

Is your community or city immune from crime? Are residents 100% safe as they go about their daily life at home, at work, or in their neighborhood? Is the place they call home and other personal property completely secure from burglars and vandals? Sadly, the plain reality of the world we live in today means the answers to these questions is no. Why is this? Sociological and psychological explanations abound, but here we take a much more basic and logical look at why crime occurs.

Crime Analysis

Research and analysis in the area of environmental criminology led to the development of a simple graphic known as the Crime Triangle, also referred to as the problem analysis triangle. The theory behind the crime triangle, called the Routine Activity Theory, also involves understanding crime situations and the importance of people who manage places.[3] This theory states that a crime occurs when a *"likely offender* and *suitable target* come together in *time and place*, without a capable guardian present."[4] Potential offenders locate what they perceive to be vulnerable targets and places and commit a criminal act, or victims interact with potential offenders but do not augment precautionary steps to deter criminal activity. It should be noted that the theory behind the crime triangle can be applied to any range of offense, from a noise complaint to rape and murder.

---

[3] This crime science paradigm was developed by Marcus Felson, Lawrence E. Cohen, and John E. Eck.

[4] http://www.popcenter.org/learning/60steps/index.cfm?stepNum=8

Figure 1.1. Problem Analysis Triangle, also known as the Crime Triangle

How does a crime fit into the model presented in the triangle? Consider this crime: A female townhouse resident parks her car in a dark, empty parking lot and is mugged by someone who has been hiding in the nearby bushes. The three crime elements of target, place, and offender come together as follows:

- Target/victim: Townhouse resident
- Place: Dark parking lot
- Offender: Person hiding in the bushes

Simply put, if you eliminate one of these elements, the crime will not occur. If the resident never drives into the parking lot, the offender is left hiding in the bushes and does not commit the crime. If the parking lot is well lit, dark of night is not an issue and no crime occurs. If there are no bushes near the townhouse, there is no place for the mugger to hide, and no crime occurs.

Figure 1.1 also depicts an outer triangle. This represents people and community factors capable of exercising control or authority over one of the three crime elements: the offender's handler, the manager of the place where a crime could occur, and the guardian of either the target or the victim.

An offender's handler is someone who knows the offender, such as the person's parents, friends, or spouse. The place element is controlled by a manager. In a multifamily housing environment, the manager could be a property owner or manager, or a landlord. The controller for the third element of target/victim is an appropriate guardian. For purposes of this book, the guardian is the police or a private security service.

When the handler of the offender has no control over the offender's behavior, or when management of the location is ineffective, or when there is no guardian present to watch over the target/victim, crime occurs. But crime can be deterred, if not eliminated, altogether by removing one or more of the three inside elements and also by ensuring the presence of one of the controlling entities.

Continuing with the same crime example, if the offender's mother insists he stay home that night, no crime occurs. If the property management company installs additional lighting in the parking lot, no crime occurs. If security patrols the parking lot at the time the resident parks her car and goes into her home, no crime occurs.

Every incident of crime can be logically analyzed the same way. Use the problem analysis triangle to match the components of a crime to the crime before, during, and after the crime occurs. When you perform this exercise, a picture of how the opportunity for a problem to occur comes clearly into focus. Equally clear, then, should be practical solutions to fix or avoid the problem.

Common Sense Works Too

Even without the crime triangle analysis, people can still improve their odds against becoming a victim of crime. The market is replete with expensive high-tech devices that enhance security, and homeowners and renters can spend a lot of money for these gadgets. People can also convert regular household items into low-tech security devices and employ common sense ideas to minimize their risk. Every step they take toward making their homes and day-to-day environments more secure means they improve their chances of keeping crime at bay.

> *Always be vigilant for threats. Don't be an easy target for a criminal. Know your surroundings; travel throughout your areas with a sense of purpose and confidence that you know where you are and where you're going; secure your personal property as well as you can and communicate with your fellow residents when something out of the ordinary is noticed. Paying attention to what looks normal on a day-to-day basis will allow you to notice when something or someone is out of the ordinary.*

Statistics abound on the types of crimes committed and the geographic location in which crimes occur. Trusted and respected agencies such as the Federal Bureau of Investigation and the Bureau of Justice provide annual reports that include national and state breakdowns of crime statistics.

Crime Reporting

In 1929, the FBI's Uniform Crime Reporting (UCR) program came into existence as the nation's source for reliable, uniform crime statistics. Since 1930, the FBI has been collecting and publishing crime data through a variety of publications. Today the FBI makes their reports available via direct download from their website (www.ucr.fbi.gov).

The Bureau of Justice and the FBI collect and define data differently. The FBI breaks out geographic area crime reporting by county type (rural, urban, suburban) and city population, or both. The UCR receives its data from some 18,000 law enforcement agencies including city, county, state, and federal law enforcement, as well as tribal and university/college law enforcement, and reports on crime where it actually occurred.

The Bureau of Justice Statistics provides geographic statistics based on rural, urban, and suburban areas, and receives its data from the National Crime Victim Survey (NCVS). The NCVS collects data directly from crime victims, who may report incidents that were never reported to police. Another key difference is that the location of these crimes is designated based on the residence of the victim, and not necessarily where the crime occurred.

The end result is that, regardless of the agency that reports crime statistics, crime rates between metropolitan/urban areas and suburban/rural areas differ. And where crime rates are higher in some areas than in others, that dynamic also creates differences in how law enforcement responds to crime and supports victims.

Crime Trends

For purposes of this general discussion, we examine FBI data only. The FBI breaks crime statistics into two main categories: violent crime and property crime. Violent crime includes four offenses: murder and nonnegligent manslaughter, rape (according to both revised and legacy definitions),[5] robbery, and aggravated assault. Property crime includes burglary, larceny-theft without force or threat against victims, motor vehicle theft, and arson.[6]

Most of us want to know if crime is on the rise and, if so, where. The answer to that question is not easy, given the distinctions in the types of crime and how crime is reported. Twenty-year crime trends indicate that violent and property crimes remain at record low numbers across the country. This trend holds true even as the number of violent crimes being committed is on the rise. For example, in the first three months of 2016, homicide rates nationwide increased 9%. Some cities experienced a significant rise in the murder rate, while others saw either a decline or drop in the rate.[7] According to Crime in America.Net[8], violent crime is on the rise in the United States as seen by crime data reported to the police and the fact that violent crime rarely increases for just a single year.

Fear of crime is also on the rise, reportedly at a 15-year high, with some 53% of adults saying they worry "a great deal" about crime and violence.[9]

In September 2016, the FBI released its national data on crime for

---

[5] According to the FBI, a new definition of rape went into effect on January 1, 2013. Depending on how individual states collect rape data, the crime is classified under either the new definition of rape or the legacy definition. A Frequently Asked Questions document is available at: https://ucr.fbi.gov/recent-program-updates/new-rape-definition-frequently-asked-questions.

[6] Arson statistics are not included in the data presented here.

[7] http://www.nytimes.com/interactive/2016/05/13/us/document-violent-crime-data.html?_r=1

[8] http://www.crimeinamerica.net/crime-rates-united-states/

[9] Ibid.

2015.[10] The figures represent crimes reported by law enforcement to the Uniform Crime Reporting program. The following tables compare overall 2014 and 2015 violent crime and property crime statistics in the United States. Data includes the year-over-year percent increase or decrease.[11]

Table 1.1

2015 Violent Crime Totals in the United States

Year	Population	Number	Rate per 100,000
2014	318.9M	1,153,022	361.6
2015	321.4M	1,197,704	372.6
% change		+3.9	+3.1

Table 1.2

2015 Property Crime Totals in the United States

Year	Population	Number	Rate per 100,000
2014	318.9M	8,209,010	2,574.1
2015	321.4M	7,993,631	2,487.0
% change		-2.6	-3.4

One explanation for the increase in violent crimes, in particular the homicide rate, could be the result of the public's increased focus and scrutiny on police officers—who may now be implementing a

[10] https://www.fbi.gov/news/stories/latest-crime-statistics-released

[11] Data retrieved from the Uniform Crime Reporting page of the FBI website. Note: The data is for illustrative purposes only and is not indicative of the efficacy or one law enforcement agency over another.

slowdown, or de-policing, for fear of backlash and rebuke.[12]

Table 1.3

Violent Crimes of Murder and Nonnegligent Manslaughter, Robbery, and Aggravated Assault in the United States

	Murder and Nonnegligent Manslaughter		**Robbery**		**Aggravated Assault**	
Year	**Number**	**Rate per 100K**	**Number**	**Rate per 100K**	**Number**	**Rate per 100K**
2014	14,164	4.4	322,905	101.3	731,089	229.2
2015	15,696	4.9	327,374	101.9	764,449	237.8
% change	+10.8	+10.0	+1.4	+0.6	+4.6	+3.7

Table 1.4

Violent Crimes of Rape (both revised and legacy definitions) in the United States

	Rape (revised definition)		**Rape (legacy definition)**	
Year	**Number**	**Rate per 100,000**	**Number**	**Rate per 100,000**
2014	118,027	37.0	84,864	26.6
2015	124,047	38.6	90,185	28.1
% change	+5.1	+4.3	+6.3	+5.4

[12] http://www.nytimes.com/2016/05/14/us/murder-rates-cities-fbi.html

Table 1.5

Property Crimes of Burglary, Larceny-Theft, Motor Vehicle Theft in the United States

	Burglary		Larceny-theft		Motor vehicle theft	
Year	**Number**	**Rate per 100K**	**Number**	**Rate per 100K**	**Number**	**Rate per 100K**
2014	1,713,153	537.2	5,809,054	1,821.5	686,803	215.4
2015	1,579,527	491.4	5,706,346	1,775.4	707,758	220.2
% change	-7.8	-8.5	-1.8	-2.5	+3.1	+2.2

Even though statistics show an increase year over year in the number of violent crimes, other statistics dropped. Any drop in the crime rate is good, but crime remains pervasive in our country. This data is not intended to scare you, but to make you more aware that crime still presents a very real threat to people no matter where they live.

Let's now look at the 2015 numbers a different way. Some crimes, in particular murders, get more news attention than others, in part because the story behind the crime involved a real-life situation that captured the attention of the news outlets and the public—in other words, drama. Everyone knows drama sells. But the real drama lies in the huge numbers of crimes other than murder that are being committed. Nearly eight million property crimes occurred in 2015, with losses tallying an astounding $14.3 billion.

Table 1.6
Numbers of Violent Crimes and Property Crimes Reported in 2015

Type of Crime	Number Committed
Murder and nonnegligent manslaughter	15,696
Robbery, aggravated assault, rape	1,215,870
Property crimes of burglary, larceny-theft, motor vehicle theft	7,993,361

Equally astounding is that these numbers reflect only major crimes. They do not show the millions of other crimes that are maintained in police records or the millions upon millions of crimes for which no one has ever been arrested. Also clear is the fact that property crimes far outnumber murder and other violent crimes. And when the millions of other crimes are factored in, the difference in numbers is even more striking.

Interestingly—and sadly—the police are unaware of much of the crime that is committed. This is because countless victims never report crimes that have been committed against them. Why? The reasons victims do not report their issue to police vary. One reason is that they report their crime to another authority, such as a guard or other official. Another reason is because the victim does not feel the crime is worth reporting, such as the petty theft of an item that may be reimbursed by insurance. Some people are afraid or ashamed to report their crime, worried about retaliation or what others, such as parents, will think or say. Lastly, some crimes go unreported because the victim simply does not trust the process or rely in its effectiveness. Consider these additional statistics from 2015.[13]

[13] https://www.bjs.gov/content/pub/pdf/cv15.pdf

Table 1.7

Percentages of Crimes Reported in 2015, as per the Bureau of Justice Statistics

Type of Crime	% Reported	% Unreported
Violent crime: rape, robbery, assault, domestic/stranger violence, violent crime with injury	47%	53%
Serious violent crime: domestic/stranger violence, violent crime with weapons or injury	55%	45%
Property crime: burglary, motor vehicle theft, theft	35%	65%

Law enforcement cannot be in all places at all times. Geographic differences and budgetary constraints are just two factors that explain why some areas receive less law enforcement protection than others. More often than not, police operate primarily in reactive mode, responding only when a call for help is made. Local police presence in our daily lives is becoming more and more a thing of the past. Gone are the days of the friendly cop on the street corner greeting passersby and helping the elderly cross the street. Today's glimpses of the local police force occur when we see them whiz by in their cars with sirens blaring.

As discussed earlier in this chapter, crime often occurs when conditions are ripe. What does that mean? That means there is a likely offender, a fitting target, and no capable guardian to preempt the offense from occurring.[14] A guardian can be anyone from police officer to security guard to ordinary citizen or resident going about their routine business. Homeowners are usually the best guardians for their own property.

---

[14] As noted in *Crime and Everyday Life*, Fifth Edition, by Marcus Felson and Mary Eckert, 2016.

> *A guardian is not usually someone who brandishes a gun or threatens an offender with quick punishment, but rather someone whose mere presence serves as a gentle reminder that someone is looking. The absence of a guardian is very important when offenders and targets are present.*[15]

Defensible Space Theory

Most criminals are opportunists who just want to get something they perceive of value without having to work too hard for it. Burglars, for example, say they will break into low-risk, easy-to-enter properties. They look for external environmental cues and activity, such as if their targeted property and the neighboring properties are occupied.

Architect and city planner Oscar Newman devised what is known as the defensible space theory. In his book, *Defensible Space: Crime Prevention Through Urban Design* (1972), Newman theorized that an "area is safer when people feel a sense of ownership and responsibility for [their] piece of a community" and that the "criminal is isolated because his turf is removed" when a responsible party owns and cares for their own space.[16] Newman made four distinctions in the types of space that exist: private, semiprivate, semipublic, and public.

As related to multifamily/multiunit residential settings, private space is, for example, the space inside a person's residence (your house, townhouse/condo, apartment). The space just outside your home, an apartment lobby, for example, is semiprivate. The space farther out, such as a common area in front of your townhouse, is semipublic. And lastly, public space is that which is most easily accessed by the public, such as sidewalks and streets. This space usually has no one person assigned direct responsibility for its security.

---

[15] Ibid.

[16] Wikipedia: https://en.wikipedia.org/wiki/Defensible_space_theory

The defensible space theory also says that a housing development is defensible only if tenants and residents adopt a role where they, as inhabitants, become "key agents" in ensuring their own security. To that end, property managers, landlords, and owners of multifamily residential communities should collaborate with residents, make them fully aware of building and space layout, and together consider these physical elements when devising their plan of defense against crime.

As new communities are designed, architects and planners can keep certain design elements in mind, for example:

- Establish parking availability as close to a residence as possible and assign parking permits to residents
- Require visitors to sign in and set a time limit on the duration of their stay
- Orient buildings so they face parking areas
- Avoid thick, tall landscaping elements near front doors and other building entrances
- Build parking lots so sight lines are free of obstruction

Existing communities can implement modifications to their physical design such as:

- Improving pathways and other common outside areas by using decorative paving and lighting
- Providing existing public access points with sufficient lighting, security, and visibility
- Reducing the number of public access points
- Placing video surveillance in strategic internal locations, and soliciting help from residents and/or security staff to monitor
- Ensuring all residential units have proper and adequate security devices in the form of locks, doors, and windows

Externally, state and local law enforcement should be available to assist when crime occurs; but when they are unavailable or unable to provide protection or serve as guardians, other alternatives exist. Private security firms, for example, provide guards and/or officers, both armed and unarmed, and security services to clients, with support ranging from standing guard at a single event to working 24/7 in a residential community. Who hasn't seen the aptly dubbed *rent-a-cop* patrolling a mall or standing watch at a concert? Though these guards are professionally trained, the public often stereotypes them into retired old men too slow to respond or controlling young men who couldn't pass the standard police test.

In recent years, the demand for security has risen, and today's private security firms have shattered the stereotype of the roving rent-a-cop image by providing highly trained and qualified workers. More and more, private security companies are being hired for guard and patrol services in residential settings, to protect people and their assets—their homes, vehicles, property, and belongings. For residents, they offer much needed and welcomed protection.

Questions for you to consider when you are deciding just how safe you really are:

- Where do crimes happen most often or most consistently in your environment?
- What crimes happen most consistently in your environment?
- Is there a pattern of offender, place, or target?
- What barriers are in place to change these dynamics?

Chapter 2: Residence Type and the Right Security Strategy

Homes come in every size, type, and style imaginable. Figuratively speaking, home is where we relax at the end of a long day, enjoy a home-cooked meal, celebrate the company of friends and family, and rest our head at night. Some might say that to do those things, the four surrounding walls do not matter.

Literally speaking, the physical walls we call home do matter, as they must meet our basic requirements of providing shelter, warmth, water, electricity, and safety. In this regard, our choice of home varies according to personal preference and lifestyle. Families and individuals typically consider a variety of factors when selecting a residence. These factors include age and income status; preferred geographic location, such as state and city or rural versus urban; local amenities such as restaurants, parks, and shopping; schools; crime levels; and more.

When all factors have been taken into consideration, the end result in choice of "home" is most typically one of the following:[17]

- Single-family home, including in an age-restricted community (also known as an active lifestyle community)
- Townhome or condominium
- Apartment
- Residence hall

Design, structure, and dynamics, as well as a number of the steps and strategies for providing safety and security are different, if not unique, for each type of residence.

In all cases, the individual homeowner or tenant can, and should, take common sense measures to ensure their own safety within their residence. Examples include keeping doors and windows locked at all times, keeping valuables out of plain sight, and checking peepholes before opening doors to strangers. Property managers and landlords will find more comprehensive lists of recommended security measures in subsequent chapters of this book.

Residences that are part of a larger community or development—multifamily communities or dwellings—have additional security

[17] Other residence types, not addressed in this book, include houseboats, mobile homes, and institution-type residences such as nursing homes.

needs. Some of these communities are gated, fenced, or walled, and employ sophisticated entry and exit mechanisms and closed-circuit TV systems. Some communities hire professional security guards to manage the flow of people and vehicles that enter the community and also to conduct security patrols on foot or in designated vehicles.

Those who own and manage these properties owe residents and tenants a safe living environment. Their responsibilities extend beyond the front entrance to also include exterior elements, such as parking lots, recreation areas, swimming pools, fitness centers, meeting rooms or clubhouses, laundry facilities, and trash and recycling areas, as well as interior building elements including elevators, stairwells, storage rooms, and hallways.

The key to adequate and appropriate security is to understand the environment—both the community itself and the surrounding neighborhoods in general. By fully understanding where and how people live, property managers, homeowner associations, and landlords possess the backbone for establishing and putting necessary and proper security measures into place.

Security in Layers

Physical security incorporates the concept of security in layers. What does that mean as it relates to multifamily residential communities where the physical security of people and property is top priority? In essence, layered security exists where building owners, property managers, and landlords have combined multiple controls to protect and lessen the potential for crime to occur. Layers of physical protective measures are put in place to prevent or mitigate unauthorized access, harm, or destruction of property.[18]

---

[18] From *Effective Physical Security*, Fourth Edition, by Lawrence J. Fennelly, 2013, Elsevier, Waltham, MA

When deciding the most appropriate security measures or layers to implement, keep in mind the assets that need to be protected; the location of those assets; and the risks, threats, and vulnerabilities they face, as this is the only way to determine an optimum level of protection. When you know and understand the people and the environment, you can provide appropriate and adequate levels of protection for each element.

The outer perimeter, or outer layers, of a community or property include various aspects where security measures can be applied. In general, they are elements that lead up to building walls and are not controlled by the residents of the community. These include: the grounds on which the building sits; the roadways within the community and if they are private or public; structural external barriers such as fences, gates, walls, etc. that prohibit or limit access; natural external barriers such as bodies of water and terrain that is difficult to negotiate; buildings and doors; parking areas; lighting; and miscellaneous openings such as sewage drains and HVAC ducts.

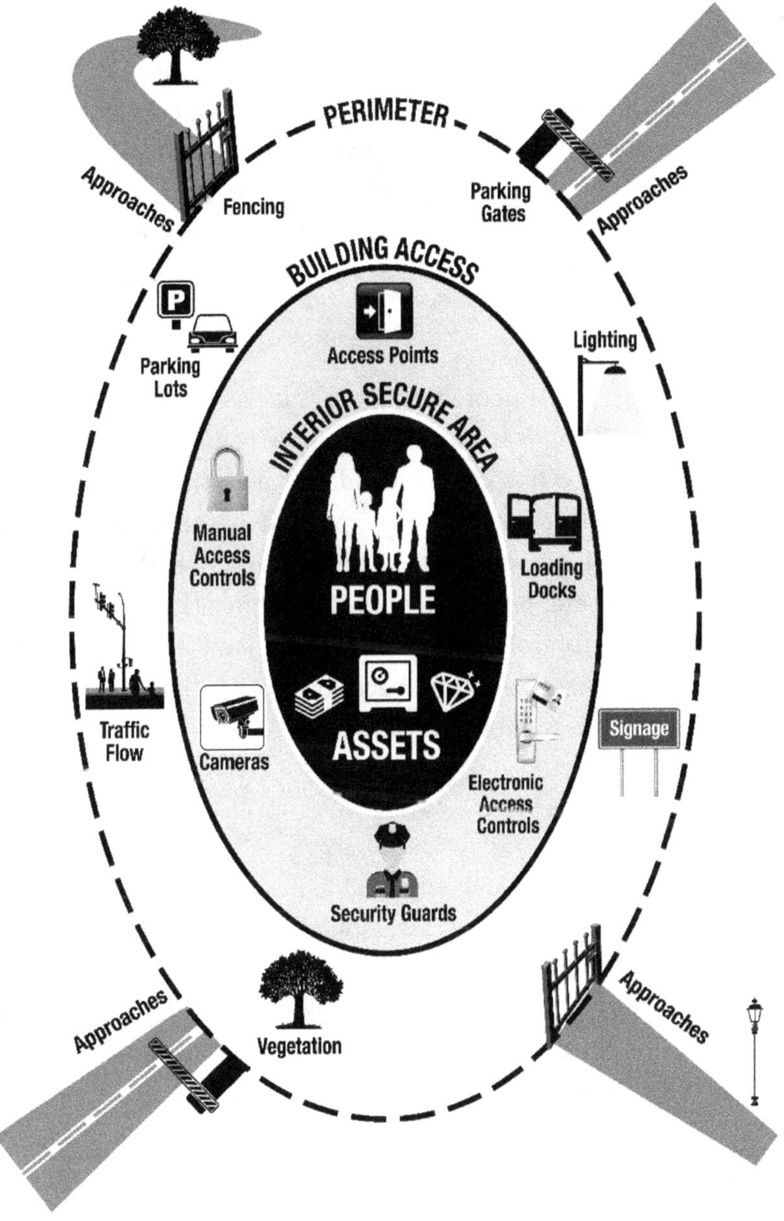

Figure 2.1. Security in Layers – depicts the layers around and within a community where security measures can be applied.

The inner layers of a property refer to internal access controls, those elements over which residents can exercise control. Security and protection should keep all of the following in mind: doors and windows, including the type of glass used on each; door locks, keys, and combinations; roofs and roof access; and other rooms or facilities within a building or on property. Access controls should keep in mind *who* and *what* access the property besides the residents: vehicles, employees of the property, contractors, delivery services, guests, and other nonresidents.

Security is best implemented in layers, but is enhanced when the layers have both *depth* and *breadth*. Defense in depth and breadth is a security strategy that uses redundancy and different measures across many access points to stop crime or at least buy time to allow for synchronized reporting and a timely response. Walls, fences, gates, signs, vegetation, cameras, security officers, security patrol vehicles, access control doors, foyers, and good lighting all work in tandem with other specialized security tools to help defend and secure property in depth and breadth.

Security Assessment

A good first step to making any multifamily residential community safe is to perform a security assessment. A security assessment is critical to identify the strengths in the existing environment and also those areas where a community is weak and vulnerable to threats and security breaches. High-quality, thorough assessments are conducted on-site, and consider security as it pertains to:

- People's physical safety
- The community's physical environment
- Electronic components
- Security and safety procedures

Keeping in mind the notion of applying security in layers, the professionals selected to inspect and report on areas of security concern in any type of multifamily residence should include the following elements:[19]

1. General use and purpose of the building – Who has access to it and when? How do people gain access? Who's responsible for building maintenance? Who has overall responsibility for the building and its security?

2. Hazards and potential hazards (e.g., crime events) that involve the building and/or its occupants.

3. How police or security officer presence applies from a crime/crime prevention standpoint. Is it operationally effective? Is it cost effective?

4. Recommendations for improvements and changes to the physical environment.

---

[19] Ibid.

5. Storage – of building elements and contents, resident belongings.

6. Recommendations for locks, key control, application of card control.

7. Alarms, closed circuit TV, portable/temporary alarm devices – analysis of when/where/how to use and cost-effectiveness.

8. Unauthorized entry and activity, and adequate signage - "No Trespassing," "No Solicitation," "Resident Parking Only," "No Loitering," "No Skateboarding," "Resident Use Only" (for example at a pool or other recreational facility).

In some cases, law enforcement officials may be available to conduct a security assessment. However, cities and towns' limited budgets and personnel mean these officials may no longer be an available resource to their local community.

In the absence of law enforcement performing a security assessment, some property managers or homeowner associations/boards attempt to conduct their own. This step, however, is not advisable. Too much is at risk. Property managers and landlords should instead look to other equally qualified professionals to conduct their security assessment and inspection. A reputable security company is the most informed, equipped, and trained to assess the status of security in multifamily communities and make recommendations for needed improvements.

These security professionals have up-to-date knowledge on crime levels and criminal behavior in the area, including the types of crimes being committed and the numbers of each type. Professionals also understand other dangers such as terrorism and civil protests, all very real and very relevant in today's world. The fee paid for the services of a professional security company to conduct a security audit will be money well spent, as the pros have seen it all and know the exact steps to take, who to interview, what questions to ask, when to evaluate, and which documents to collect and review.

Property managers and homeowner associations who design security strategies and implement tactics based on the recommendations of a professional assessment provide the residents in their community a first defense against burglars, thieves, and vandals. At a minimum, they improve their community's odds against falling victim to these criminal elements and possibly deter crime altogether.

Security professionals often suggest that a good first step is to change perspective. Rather than approach security from the perspective of property manager or landlord, look at the safety and security of your community through the eyes of a criminal. From there, design security strategies and implement tactics to stave off crime.

Whether a community is looking for a full-time professional security company to guard their community or they're interested in having an in-depth security audit performed, homeowner associations and property managers should look for a company that knows the community, has the expertise and experience to do a thorough job using current technology and information, and that truly cares about the property and those who reside there.

Questions for you to consider when devising the best security strategy for your residence type:

- When is the last time you had a property security assessment?
- What do you consider your most valuable asset?
- What do others see or experience on your property that you might miss?

Chapter 3: Apartments

The benefits to living in an apartment are many. Renters are free of the obligation to perform repairs and maintenance; they have access to a suite of amenities such as a swimming pool and fitness center; and they can enjoy a convenient lifestyle in the neighborhood of their choice. Another advantage apartment dwellers enjoy is an enhanced sense of security. Depending on the type and location of the apartment complex, residents may have multiple layers of security from gates at the entrance to alarms on each apartment.

Freddie Mac, the federal government's home loan mortgage corporation, defines multifamily rental housing types[20] as follows.

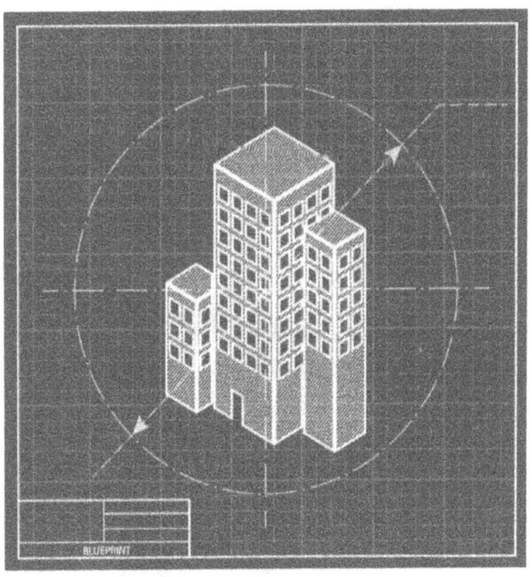

- High-rise – A building with nine or more floors and at least one elevator.
- Mid-rise – A multistory building with at least one elevator.
- Garden – A one-, two-, or three-story building, with or without an elevator, part of a larger complex in a

[20] Freddie Mac defines multifamily as five or more units. Available here: http://www.freddiemac.com/blog/rental_housing/20150727_apartment_property_types.html

garden-like setting; some apartments can be at or below ground level.

- Walk-up – A multi-story building with no elevator.

The different types of apartment buildings and complexes present their own requirements and challenges when it comes to keeping residents safe. Landlords and property and building managers must make safety and security a priority. They have a certain amount of responsibility—and liability—to ensure a safe environment for their tenants and, often, landlord-tenant laws provide the legal obligation for them to take all reasonable precautions to do just that.

Good tenants hate being disturbed, whether by a noisy party, people coming or going in the course of drug sales, a loud TV, screaming kids, maintenance issues—whatever the cause. When they come home to their own castle, they prefer not to be disturbed.

This notion is underscored in a March 2016 article at website *the balance*. The article, entitled "9 Reasons Why Tenants Leave a Rental,"[21] explains reason #6: They leave because of problems with a neighbor.

> *Some tenants will move due to issues with neighbors or other tenants. They may have noise complaints, feel unsafe around a neighbor or constantly butt heads with another individual for whatever reason. A tenant wants to be able to enjoy their home in peace. If they don't feel their home is a sanctuary, they are more likely to leave.*

Beyond the legalities, providing a safe, welcoming environment is good for business. Prospective tenants will always keep safety at or near top of list when searching for an apartment, and avoid communities with high rates of burglaries and vandalism or where management displays no apparent concern for the safety of those who live in the community.

---

[21] https://www.thebalance.com/reasons-tenants-leave-rental-2125040

> *Your vehicle is not a storage location for valuables, unless you're okay with them disappearing.*

More and more, landlords of rental apartment communities understand the need to make apartment security a priority—not just for existing residents and the property, but also to attract new tenants.

One way managers and landlords show they take safety seriously is to provide a security team comprised, in essence, of in-house employees who act as guards. At first glance, this step may appease building managers from a cost perspective while also providing the appearance of a layer of security to residents. The reality is, cost effectiveness flies out the window when the costs of training, uniforms, scheduling, and management of the team are

> *Make sure renters understand the apartment rules and regulations upon signing their lease.*

calculated. A further cost not usually factored in is that of the management company being held liable for complaints, civil or otherwise, regarding an action involving an in-house security guard. Proper response and resolution of these complaints likely also includes legal fees the property manager will need to incur.

Another solution to the question of having a security presence is to hire an outside security firm, a step that eliminates the personnel management and other miscellaneous issues of using an in-house security company. Property managers can hand *every detail* related to the security of their property and residents over to the security company, who will provide officers, manage personnel and scheduling matters, and be responsible for responding to complaints. The presence of patrol vehicles and uniformed guards provides existing and potential residents peace of mind and deters would-be criminals. At a minimum, an outside security firm will patrol the parking lots and buildings, and check all other facilities and amenities such as laundry and recreation.

> *Be aware of your surroundings. Park in well-lit areas. Report lights out and other matters requiring maintenance or repair.*

A good security firm will provide fully trained security officers who are equipped to handle virtually any issue that may arise. These officers will wear a readily recognizable uniform and may be armed or unarmed. Their presence on a property, combined with patrol vehicles outfitted with identifying reflective graphics will serve as a strong visual deterrent against crime and criminals.

Truth that Is Stranger than Fiction

One night, one of my supervisors came upon a woman sleeping in her driver's seat in the parking lot of one of our communities. When the supervisor knocked on the car window, the lady started screaming and backed out of the spot at a high rate of speed. On the video replay, you could hear my supervisor say, "Don't hit my truck." The woman parked in a spot just a couple of hundred feet away and tried to go back to sleep. Funny, scary, and a head-shaker all in one.

Technology, too, plays an equally important role. A top-notch security company will employ Wi-Fi capabilities for communicating and for responding promptly to calls. Vehicles will be GPS equipped so managers know where they are at all times. And reports and other messaging will be date and time-stamped so property managers can verify performance and activity.

Just Another Routine Day for a Patrol Officer? Not Exactly.

Officer H. was conducting a roving vehicle patrol through one of our multifamily complexes around 2 a.m. and noticed four men shove another person inside a car and drive off. Officer H. contacted the local police as he followed the vehicle through the client's property. Just as the suspects' vehicle turned out of sight to leave the property, one of the men inside the vehicle shot another in the chest. The driver ditched the vehicle just down the road and two primary suspects jumped out and ran away from the scene. Officer H. had turned the corner just in time for his vehicle's dash camera to film the actions of the two suspects.

Officer H. was unaware one of the men had been shot, but observed him stumbling out of the vehicle and falling into the street. Officer H. was still on the phone with the police and reported everything to them as it happened. He drove to the scene and asked if everything was okay. Two of the individuals that had remained onsite informed Officer H. of the third who had been shot. Officer H. immediately updated the police. Then, with complete disregard for his own safety and not knowing anything about the men who stayed behind or their intentions, Officer H. left his vehicle and rendered first aid to the injured young man, providing comfort until the paramedics arrived. For the following seven hours, he worked with a detective task force to help build the case, providing details that led to understanding what actually took place and a baseline description of the individuals who committed the crime. Officer H.'s actions reflected great credit upon himself and the Signal 88 organization. We are very proud to have him as part of our team.

Questions for you to consider when you are deciding the best security strategy for your apartment complex:

- What environmental concerns affect tenants' peace of mind?
- Do you regularly survey tenants on concerns they may have regarding community and personal safety?
- How might tenant concerns regarding safety affect their desire to remain in your community?

Below you will find helpful lists landlords and property managers can share with tenants to help them keep personal and community property safe.

General Apartment Security Tips

- Regardless of where you go on the property, inside or out, be consciously aware of your surroundings at all times. Remain alert and pay attention to specific areas of the building you live in: hallways, stairwells, storage rooms, and laundry rooms. Outside, be alert in parking and trash areas, and common areas that include pools and sports and recreational facilities.

- Control your personal space inside the apartment—your bedroom—by establishing a barrier between you and any potential threat. For example, you can purchase a door stop that doubles as an alarm that goes off when an intruder enters. The cost for this easy type of security is approximately $10. Another type of barrier is a door pole that wedges into place from the floor to door handle. When you have these simple types of barriers in place, you have time to react appropriately, such as by calling the police or security company.

- Apartment roommates should set an agreement upfront regarding each other's guests. Do you trust who he or she brings into the apartment? Respect each other's wishes regarding who is permitted to stay overnight or remain in the apartment while their host is not present. Statistics show that the overwhelming majority of attacks happen by someone the victim knows.

- Set ground rules when multiple roommates move in together on how they will keep their apartment and each other safe. Mutual respect for each other and each other's property should make obtaining buy-in easy. These types of agreements represent a best defense against crime.

- Call 911 and/or your building manager immediately to report suspicious behavior or activity.

- Get to know your neighbors and know where they live. When you can identify the rightful residents, you can more easily spot a real intruder.

- As much as possible, use only well-lit sidewalks, doorways, hallways, and stairways. Report insufficient or malfunctioning lighting to your property manager for repair.

- Do not step onto an elevator if you feel uncomfortable or are suspicious of another person on the elevator. Stand near the elevator control buttons and know which is the emergency button.

General Apartment Security Tips When at Home

- Before moving in, make sure the locks to your unit have been changed.

- Your main door should have a deadbolt lock and peephole so you can see who is outside your unit.

- If your apartment does not already have a built-in security system, purchase a small security unit you can place on a door and set it to go off when there is an unauthorized entry.

- *Never* open your door to a stranger, no matter what they request. If necessary, call 911 or the property manager on the person's behalf, but do so from inside your locked apartment.

- List only your last name or first initial and last name on mailbox or intercom directory.

- Fit sliding glass doors and windows with appropriate auxiliary locking devices.

- First-floor and lower units should have additional security on the windows that prevent a burglar from raising the window and entering. A simple dowel placed vertically at one edge of a window prevents the window from being opened. Just make sure you can easily remove the dowel yourself if you need to use the window as an escape route in the event of an emergency.

- Engrave and/or document a list of all items of value, and keep the list in a separate safe location.

General Apartment Security Tips When You Go Out

- Lock all doors and windows.
- When you return home, and something is amiss or you think someone is inside, don't go in. Call 911, Security, or the manager, and wait with a neighbor for help to arrive.
- At night, put TVs and lamps on a variety of timers set to go on and off at different times.
- Don't hide your spare key in what you think is your secret hiding place somewhere outside your unit; burglars are experts at finding people's secret hiding places. Let a trusted neighbor keep your spare key for you.
- Don't tempt burglars by leaving expensive or valuable items visible through windows or doors.

Laundry Room Safety

- Is the lighting in the laundry room bright, and is the room clean and in good working order?
- If the laundry area is in a separate building, are the paths to the area clear, open, well lit, and visible?
- Is there a large mirror angled for residents who want to enter the laundry room to clearly see if anyone is inside before they enter?
- Is the laundry room door lockable from the inside? Does it include a proper panic bar/handle? Does the window on the door

contain metal mesh to prevent someone from breaking the glass and unlocking the door from the outside?

- Consider doing laundry with a friend or neighbor (in pairs) – for safety in numbers.

Safety at Community Amenities

- Are common areas, fitness/sporting areas, recreation areas, and the pool designated as for use only by residents and their invited guests?

- Do not go into common areas or recreational facilities if you are suspicious of one or more people already using the facility.

- Avoid areas where lighting is insufficient or malfunctioning; report the issue to the manager.

- Leave your jewelry, cash, wallet, and other valuables in your locked apartment.

Safety in Parking Lots

- Park as close to your unit as possible, in a well-lit area.

- Lighting in the parking lot should be bright; if lighting is deficient or faulty, report it to the manager.

- Parking spaces should not be identified with the same unit number/letter as the apartment or condo to make it difficult for burglars to target units where they believe no one is home.

- Do not leave any items visible on the seats of your car or elsewhere. A burglar might think your $15 sunglasses are actually worth $200, and break in a window to steal them.

- Take advantage of all available car alarm devices and anti-theft technology.
- Whether your car is parked at your own apartment complex or elsewhere, always lock it and keep your keys in your possession.

Chapter 4: Townhome Communities and Condominiums

Townhome and condominium living provides a great many benefits to people who are looking for a community-type lifestyle as an alternative to living in a single-family home. Minimal yardwork; amenities such as pools and playgrounds, fitness centers, and community gathering rooms; and association rules (bylaws, covenants and restrictions) combine to afford residents easy, convenient living and a sense of community. In spite of community-type living, differences do exist between condos and townhomes.

In a townhome, residents:

- Own their unit from top to bottom (roof to basement)
- Enter directly from the outside
- Probably live on multiple levels and have a basement
- Usually have a deck or patio for outdoor living

- May have an attached garage or parking space out front
- Share at least one side wall with a neighbor
- Pay an association fee for set services

In a condo, residents:

- Own the condo itself plus an interest in common elements (e.g., the roof and exterior walls) as defined by governing documents
- Share the entryway and hallways with neighbors
- Probably live on a single level in a multilevel building
- May have parking in detached garages or open stalls
- Might share laundry facilities with neighbors
- Pay a condo fee to cover amenities and common element expenses

One benefit to living in a condo or townhouse community is that residents perceive a greater sense of safety and security. This view can hold true in both gated and non-gated communities, from plain and simple to high-end luxury. Because neighbors live in such close proximity, they are readily available to help each other out. They also tend to notice unusual activity or noise, and pay closer attention when an unknown person or people are present.

> *Get involved with your community and get to know your neighbors.*

In spite of the security townhome and condo residents say they feel, their sense of security could be false, as communities and individual homes within them are still subject to crime, including burglaries, break-ins, vehicle theft, and vandalism. Vigilance is key, given the number of nonresidents who are in and out of communities on a daily basis: independent contractors and repair companies, delivery trucks, landscapers, garbage collectors, and acquaintances of the residents. The potential for a breach in a community's security is real. The FBI's 2015 crime statistics indicate a nationwide estimate of 7,993,631 property crimes, with a decrease in burglaries and larceny-thefts from the previous year, but an increase in the number of motor vehicle thefts. 2015 also saw an estimated 1,197,704 violent crimes, with the numbers of both murder and non-negligent manslaughter increased from 2014.[22]

Ensure homeowners keep their condos and the entire community up to standards from a security perspective.

Property management companies and homeowner/condo associations must keep homeowner and resident security a top priority, and take reasonable steps to protect them, their property, and the community as a whole, from injury and from legal liability. Residents will feel a higher degree of satisfaction when they know their interests in both their safety as well as property are being cared for. And this, too, protects the financial investment homeowners have in their home and ensures a good return on that investment when it comes time to sell—a community with a solid record of safety and that is notably secure will attract more buyers than one that is not.

Lock all doors and windows when leaving and overnight.

Remove valuables from decks and balconies.

[22] These statistics represent reported crimes. Source: https://www.fbi.gov/news/pressrel/press-releases/fbi-releases-2015-crime-statistics.

How a Homeowner's Association Can Make Their Community Safer for Everyone

Community boards and homeowner associations (HOAs), in conjunction with property management companies can, and should, take all reasonable measures to ensure the safety and security of their community and its residents. Below we list practical steps HOAs can implement to make and keep community and homeowner property safe.

> *Take ownership of your community. Start a Neighborhood Watch. The more involved people are, the more they communicate. And security concerns will be less likely to go unnoticed.*

- Conduct a security survey and audit. This simple step will pay big dividends in terms of informing the HOA where security is lax or deficient throughout the community. Survey residents for their concerns, obtain input from the association management company to understand the location and value of the communities' assets, and hire a professional security company to audit the community to look for vulnerabilities and learn what could be done to deter crime.

- Determine the best security solution for the community. This will, of course, depend on the size of the property and the security concern you are trying to solve. You may want to hire a professional security company to provide a guard at a front gate and/or vehicle to patrol the entire community. Closed-circuit TV (CCTV) lets guards view and monitor activity inside buildings and elsewhere on property.

- Bushes and trees add shade and beauty to any community, but landscaping close to your building should be low to the ground and well-trimmed to prevent a person from hiding there.

- Control access to buildings and amenities within the community. Require key card access to facilities such as the fitness center or wrist tags for access to the pool. Track closely other people who may require access, such as a cleaning company or caterer, including having them sign in when they enter the community and sign out when they leave.

- Consider the need for an outside security company to provide a presence in the form of an officer or guard at the front entry or a roving patrol to monitor the entire property. These officers are professionally trained, may be armed or unarmed, and are fully equipped to handle virtually any issue that may arise. In addition, they will have a direct line to law enforcement to ensure proper and appropriate help will come when needed.

- Address front-gate issues such as tailgating, where one or more non-community vehicles enter the community on the tails of one that is authorized to enter. Research options to install the best gate for your community, including exit gates with collapsible spikes to deter wrong-way access.

- Educate homeowners. Establish a community watch program. Provide security updates in the HOA newsletter and at HOA meetings. Residents will be pleased to know steps are being taken to keep them and their homes and families safe and secure.

Criminals know an easy target when they see one. The more difficult the association and residents make it for a criminal to enter the property—whether an individual home or the property in general—the better the chances that criminal element will move on.

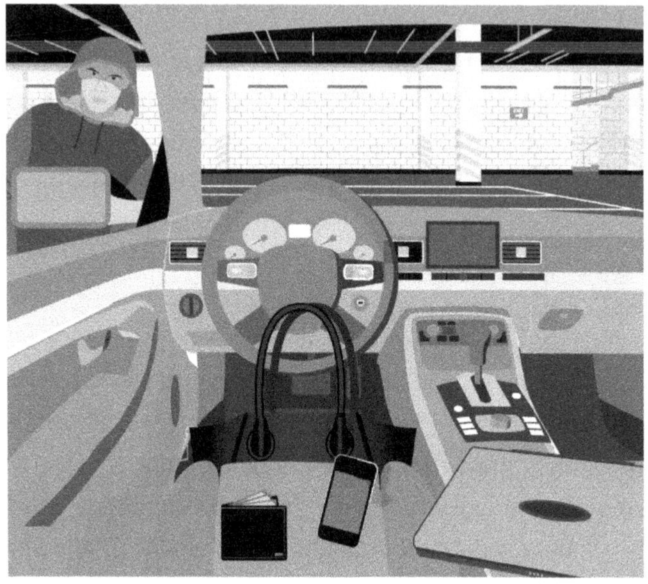

Remove all items of value from your car when parking it—computers, cell devices, cash, coins, firearms, jewelry.

Questions for you to consider when you are deciding a safety strategy for your townhome or condominium community:

- Homeowners have a vested interest in their community – How does that change how they perceive crime and its effect on property values?
- How have the community and its surroundings changed over time, and what, within the community, may need to change as a result to continue to keep residents safe?
- What is the best way to organize the community so that all safety concerns can be addressed?

Below you will find a helpful list property managers and homeowner associations can share with residents to help them keep personal and community property safe.

General Townhome Security Tips for Homeowners

- Get to know, or at least recognize, other residents in your vicinity as well as other people who are regularly in your community, such as landscapers.

- When going away for an extended period of time, let a reliable, trustworthy neighbor know. If you are comfortable, leave your contact number and a copy of your house key with them, in case they need to reach you. Or, let them know if you plan on having someone check on your home while you are away. Stop newspaper and mail delivery so these items don't back up and provide a clue that no one is at home.

- Whether you're at work for the day or away for a week, don't let package deliveries sit on your front door step unattended. If possible, have packages delivered to a neighbor's address or plan deliveries to arrive at times you know you will be home.

- Set lights in different rooms on timers so they come on and go off at different times during evening and night hours. Along with that, hang window coverings to prevent people on the outside from looking in and seeing you and your belongings at night.

- Install multiple locks on doors and bolster the strength of existing locks. Lock sets, chains, and deadbolt locks make it more difficult for would-be thieves to break in. If your door doesn't have a peephole, install one and use it every time your doorbell rings.

- Keep valuables such as jewelry and electronics out of sight. By leaving them plainly visible, you invite thieves who will steal them and sell them immediately for cash.

- Engrave and/or document a list of all items of value, and keep the list in a separate safe location.

- The next best thing to having an interior alarm system is to install specialized theft-deterrent latches to windows and patio doors. These mechanisms do more than just keep windows locked. They allow windows be open to a certain height, after which the mechanism blocks it from being opened further.

- Keep garage doors closed at all times when not in use to prevent thieves from stealing directly from your garage or gaining quick, easy entry to your home through an inside door.

- Install floodlights and/or motion-detection lighting on decks and patios and other areas or points of entry into your home or garage where general community lighting does not reach.

Chapter 5: Age-Restricted Communities

Age-restricted communities have grown in popularity in recent years. Savvy marketers rarely refer to them as *retirement* communities, but rather as *active adult* or *lifestyle* communities. The premise behind them, however, is related to age. In an age-restricted community, at least 80% of the occupied residences must have at least one person living in them who is age 55 or older, and anyone under the age of 19 is restricted from being a permanent resident. Other types of age-related communities include *age-targeted*, which market to adults age 55 and over but which are not age-restricted; and *leisure* communities, which are intended for empty nesters.

Active adult communities come in all shapes and sizes, with many focused on a particular location or lifestyle. These communities can be comprised of single-family homes; cluster homes, where residences are grouped close together and the common area is for open space or recreational purposes; townhomes; high-rise condos; manufactured homes, also referred to as mobile homes; modular homes; and even RV retirement parks. Some communities are gated, some have on-site security guards and/or patrols, and others are open for anyone to enter.

> *Know your neighbors and give one you trust the contact information for your family.*

Many age-restricted communities are designed and built in a high-end, resort-like setting with residents' needs and wants in mind. Community and activity managers promote an active lifestyle for residents, and provide a wide range of amenities such as a golf course, indoor/outdoor swimming pools, walking and biking trails, tennis courts, restaurants, clubhouse with meeting and game rooms, library/media center, exercise room, computer labs, on-site health care facilities, lakes for sailing and fishing, and more—in a word, something for everyone.

> *If your medical condition dictates, always have a way to summon medical assistance, such as a cell phone or pendant.*

Reputation of the community is important. Beyond the location and amenities afforded in age-restricted retirement communities, residents demand identification and screening of anyone who enters their community—residents and their visiting guests and family members, delivery services, and companies with whom the community does business, such as landscapers, facility cleaning services, and maintenance providers. If a security breach or violation occurs on the part of any one of the above groups of people, residents expect swift and appropriate measures be taken to address it.

The security staffing and programs should be tailored to meet both the environment and the culture of the community. Residents look for professionalism and friendliness—that is, security officers and guards must possess and provide proper levels of customer service. They must be aware of, and sensitive to, resident needs and expectations. These homeowners demand security staff members be highly trained and developed, and demonstrably capable of meeting all their and their community's specific security requirements.

Another area that matters to residents—and their families who live across town or across the country—is the well-being of the residents. This population wants to live and remain as independent and safely as possible for as long as possible. To that end, security professionals in senior living communities should be alert to issues that potentially affect those in the very community they are hired to protect: elder abuse; drug abuse; fraudulent health care practices; the ability to provide first aid, perform CPR, operate an AED, and to act as first responders in the event of an emergency.

Residents should take ownership of their community and start a Neighborhood Watch. The more involved they are with their community, the more they will communicate, and be less likely to have security concerns go unnoticed.

Officers and security managers must be available to meet with community managers and boards as needed as well as take the time to assist and escort residents when help is needed. This level of support and service can be provided when residents trust the company hired to protect them and their property. To gain that trust, officers must continually align their work, performance, and visibility to meet everyone's expectations.

Property managers and directors on the boards of homeowners' associations (HOAs) of age-restricted communities should work only with a professional security company that understands and can meet the unique needs of these communities. When selecting a company, keep in mind the following support services your particular community may need:

- Consulting to review existing levels of security and recommend improvements—a company that has experience in conducting security audits in age-restricted communities, and that will tell just how secure your community is, or is not
- Foot and vehicle patrols of the community—including checks of both residential and common areas and buildings
- Ability to assess threats to the community and its residents
- Security presence in the community's main reception area
- Visitor check-in, monitoring, and assistance, to ensure visitors reach the right destination and are tracked until they exit the property
- Escort services if requested, to ensure residents return safely to their homes
- Crisis management and the ability to respond quickly and appropriately to an emergency such as a fire, flood, or medical emergency
- Full incident reporting, to remain as transparent to the community as possible

- A proactive approach to addressing any matter relating to resident safety and security—for example, if lights in a parking area are out, promptly report the matter for repair

Property managers of age-restricted communities should also request that any outside security company they hire is capable of taking appropriate actions when fire alarms go off, has minimal response time to emergency-call situations, manages and assists with door code and key card entry, patrols parking lots and enforces parking rules, escorts ambulances on property, checks on vacant residences or those where the homeowner is away, and conducts regular safety inspections of every facility on property.

As with any type of multifamily residential community, homeowners and residents in age-restricted communities should be encouraged to get to know their neighbors and establish one or more trustworthy relationships where people support and keep an eye on each other. In addition, residents should be kept well informed of the goings-on in their community.

Homeowners' association meetings, attended by both property management and security company personnel, afford residents the opportunity to ask questions and have their concerns regarding safety in their neighborhood addressed.

Questions for you to consider when you are deciding the best security strategy for your age-restricted community:

- What different concerns do residents in age-restricted communities have, given the higher likelihood of internal crime opportunity from vendors, visitors, and others?
- How do the hours of when a crime is liable to occur change the perception of peace of mind on the property?
- How do different community behaviors change the perception of peace of mind on the property?

HOA board members, with support from their property manager, can help residents keep their community and personal property safe by sharing the below tips.

General Security Tips for Homeowners in Age-Restricted Communities

- It is easy for some people to keep to themselves and not want to get involved in the goings-on in their community. For everyone's safety and security, however, residents should get to know, or at least recognize, each other as well as other people who enter the community on a regular basis, such as landscapers.

- When traveling for an extended period, whether over a long weekend or three months over winter, let property management and a reliable, trustworthy neighbor know. If you are comfortable, leave your contact number and a copy of your house key with your neighbor, in case they need to enter your house or otherwise reach you. Or, if you plan on having someone else such as a family member check on your home while you are away, let your neighbor know exactly who will be entering your home.

- Stop newspaper and mail delivery so these items don't back up and provide a clue that no one is at home.

- Don't allow package deliveries to sit on your front door step unattended if you're away for even a day. If possible, have packages delivered to a neighbor's address or plan deliveries to arrive at times you know you will be home to receive them.

- Set lights on timers throughout your home so they come on and go off at different times during evening and night hours.

- Close blinds and drapes at night so people on the outside are unable to look in and see you or your belongings.

- Hire a locksmith to install multiple locks on doors and bolster the strength of existing locks. If you purchased the home on a resale, change the locks altogether. Lock sets, chains, and deadbolt locks make it more difficult for would-be thieves to break in.

- If your door doesn't have a peephole, install one and use it every time your doorbell rings.

- "Out of sight, out of mind." Valuables such as jewelry and electronics should be kept safely out of sight to avoid inviting thieves to break in and steal them.

- Engrave and/or document a list of all items of value, and keep the list in a separate safe location.

- Install specialized theft-deterrent latches on windows and patio doors. They are the next best thing to having an interior alarm system. Some window lock mechanisms allow windows to open only to a certain height, after which the mechanism blocks the window from being opened further.

- Unless you are pulling in or out of your garage, keep the garage door closed at all times. An open garage door is an open invitation to a thief to steal directly from your garage or gain quick, easy entry to your home through the inside door.

- Floodlights and/or motion-detection lighting installed on decks, patios, and other outside areas or points of entry into your home or garage provide additional lighting where general community lighting does not reach.

Chapter 6: Dormitories, Residence Halls, Student Housing

Every parent wants to believe their child will be safe when they send them off to school, whether school is a college-prep boarding school for teens or a four-year college or university. In recent years, the issue of security in schools and universities has received intense scrutiny in light of horrendous acts of violence that have taken place on campuses and in classrooms across our country.

Sadly, crime can, and does, occur in dormitories, residence halls, and student housing facilities of schools everywhere. Parents and students alike should be keenly concerned about safety and security in these environments, and take advantage of all available resources, including closely reviewing an institution's most recent security report as part of their decision-making process when it comes time to select a school.

Neither the student nor his or her parents should discount off-campus housing, especially apartments that are affiliated with the school, as these residential facilities are held to higher standards of security than other apartments not affiliated with the school. Gated communities, though not foolproof against crime, do provide an extra layer of protection that deters criminal activity. Prospective students and their parents should research the school's complete security guidelines and policy, their security procedures, and their code of conduct. Parents who know their child is safe have peace of mind and sleep better at night.

Advice from a security professional to students who live in a campus residence hall: This is your first time away from home. Pace yourself and don't do things that will get you in trouble.

Campus Security and the Law

Over the years, Congress has enacted a series of laws and amendments to existing laws that require most colleges and universities to report on-campus crime.[23] For example, the Crime Awareness and Campus Security Act of 1990 required all postsecondary institutions participating in federal student financial assistance programs under the Higher Education Act of 1965 to disclose security information and statistics on campus crime. This law was amended in 1998 and renamed to the Jeanne Clery Disclosure of Campus Security Policy and Campus Crime Statistics Act, known

[23] Source: The Handbook for Campus Safety and Security Reporting, 2016 Edition. Available at: http://www2.ed.gov/admins/lead/safety/handbook.pdf.

generally as the Clery Act, so named after student Jeanne Clery who was murdered inside a campus dormitory.

More recently, the Violence Against Women Reauthorization Act of 2013 (VAWA) was signed into law. This act, which includes amendments to the Clery law, requires educational institutions to make available their policies, programs, and statistics pertaining to date and domestic violence, sexual assault, stalking, and more.

The U.S. Department of Education makes checking campus crime statistics easy. Their user-friendly online tool, Campus Safety and Security (CSS),[24] allows users to select and analyze data and crime statistics for public, private, and state 2- and 4-year higher education institutions. Users can generate data for one school or many, compare statistics for multiple years, and search for results in a particular area such as criminal or VAWA offenses.

Students, though generally responsible and reliable, can also be their own worst enemy. Peer pressure, poor judgment, and any number of other unknown outside influencers can cause a young person to make a bad decision and do something they later regret. It is normal, especially for students who are away from home for the first time, to want to exercise their independence. Mom and Dad's curfew is gone, and no one is around to tell them where they can and cannot go. Suddenly, a whole new social and travel universe has opened up, and logically, students want to explore.

Whether their child is a boy or a girl, parents should not let their young adult students leave home without having "the talk" – you know, about safety and security on campus. When safety is the emphasis and students learn safety basics, they will listen, regardless of how many times they roll their eyes. And, they can take proactive

---

[24] Available at: http://ope.ed.gov/campussafety/#/.

steps to keep themselves and their residence halls safe. By applying common sense approaches and taking easy but necessary precautions, the chances of any student being victimized decrease.

- *Don't block open access doors*
- *Remove or report any exterior door found blocked open*
- *Use the buddy system or campus escort services when walking at night*
- *Stay off the phone when walking to and from your dorm*

It should be noted that not all school and campus crime is committed by students. Criminals from within the larger community will look for breaches in standard security measures, and also for unsuspecting, naïve students who appear to be unfamiliar with the ways of the world. Thieves and burglars will jump on any weakness they spot in the student's daily living habits to commit a crime against him or her.

Students—both male and female—should be educated on the topic of sexual assault and sexual harassment. They need to understand what is considered sexual assault, and the legal consequences for committing sexual assault. A large percentage of these crimes are committed by someone the student victim knows.

How to Improve Security on Campus

Colleges and universities provide security personnel and dedicate an entire department to student and campus security. Campus security services are responsible for maintaining security and responding to on-campus emergencies, and should be available 24 hours a day, 7 days a week, 365 days a year.

A good campus security company will have a visible presence on campus and in all residence halls and other student housing in the form of foot, bicycle, and vehicle patrols. They will provide a range of services, including crime handling and crime prevention, incident reporting, incident investigation, medical and fire emergency response, and more. Officers will be in continual communication with a centralized security center that is staffed around the clock to handle both emergency and routine phone calls. Campus security Is also responsible for monitoring security cameras and coordinating emergency response.

Don't be afraid to report suspicious activity.

Campus security personnel also coordinate response with local law enforcement and emergency responders as necessary. In some cases, they also collaborate with student officers involved in campus security and safety. Campuses should have strategically placed emergency phones—known as Code Blue phones—located across campus and also provide emergency call instructions for when and how students should place emergency calls. For example, for a situation that requires immediate police, fire, or medical response, students should know to call 911. For other emergency situations, students should know the number to call for campus security.

Every call placed by a student to campus security is significant and should never be dismissed. Consider a female student who needs someone to accompany her back to her dorm. A good security guard provides the requested escort, but also listens and observes along the way. The guard attempts to discover why the student requested the escort. Was it because it was dark? Was someone following her? Did she feel threatened? The guard takes in the entire situation and environment, and documents every detail in his or her security report—for example, if there were any cars or other people in the vicinity or the lighting conditions along the way. If the student's request for an escort was made because she feels unsafe and/or threatened, security will have documented the event and started a file that can be referenced later on if necessary, and even coordinated with police efforts.

How to Handle a Complaint

Invariably in the course of an academic year, a student or neighbor will place a call to campus security to make a nuisance complaint, for example, of loud noise or partying in a dorm or other student residence. These types of situations could be handled in one of two ways. One way is for security to arrive on scene, bang on doors, and yell at alleged offenders to knock off the noise. Another way is for security to approach the situation in a nonconfrontational, courteous manner and politely request the partiers turn down the noise. Which approach do you think will yield the best results?

True professionals understand that a hostile, aggressive challenge in the middle of these types of situations never achieves the desired results. Even if the guard who yells succeeds in getting the partiers to turn down their noise, the end result will potentially be a group of students who now resent the security guard and/or the person who filed the complaint. This anger can fester and cause the partiers to turn the music up even louder once they know security has moved on, or even to commit potentially dangerous future actions against complainers or security.

Professional guards know that people always react and respond more favorably when treated with respect and consideration. By making a polite request to have the music turned down, the guard establishes a connection—usually friendly—and often gets a positive response in return. Everyone saves face under these circumstances. Sometimes, the students and partiers are not even aware of how loud their party has gotten.

Guards will even respond to calls placed by the host of a party who might not have the wherewithal to control guests, a completely understandable situation. The strategy is always to promote de-escalation so that a situation does not grow any worse than it already is. An effective guard always has their conversation planned in advance, knowing that disrespectful treatment or having a knee-jerk reaction leads nowhere.

Of course, not every situation is resolved with a friendly request to turn down the music. Partying goes on, party-goers get drunk and mouth off, outsiders crash the party, and worse. Professional guards know they must handle these situations according to the circumstances or behaviors being exhibited by the people at the party. Guards know they are not police officers, but they have the ability and authority to ask the group to disperse. Once again, they treat attendees with respect and might even suggest they make the right decision by leaving—and then wait until they do so, or call the police to take control of the situation.

Professional security guards take their job of protecting people and property seriously. A calm, respectful approach is the best technique to de-escalate a situation. College campuses and communities are soft targets for criminal activity. Students are busy with studies and other activities, and few are used to living on their own.

Questions for you to consider when you are deciding the best security strategy for a dormitory, residence hall, or off-campus housing complex:

- With a higher likelihood of multiple lease signors on each residence, how are the needs and liabilities of the community affected?
- What seasonal variations occur on these properties throughout the year that may affect security needs?

Below you will find helpful lists school administrators, landlords, and property managers can share with students to help them keep personal and community property safe.

General Security Tips for Students in On-campus Residence Halls and Off-campus Housing

- Familiarize yourself with the on-campus security company and know how to reach them from any location. Program the emergency phone number for campus security into your cell phone.

- Know who your Resident Advisor (RA) is as well as the location of the RA's room.

- Lock the door to your room when sleeping and anytime you leave, even if just to use the bathroom.

- Remain with your guests at all times. You are responsible for your guests and their actions. By escorting them, you not only track their actions, you let other students in the dorm know that your guest is authorized to be in the building.

- Do not let strangers into the building. Inform the unknown person he or she needs to call the person they are visiting, and that person will come to let them in. Or, ask the stranger who they have come to see and let that fellow student know they have a visitor waiting at the front door.

- If you see an unescorted person walking around the residence hall, approach and ask them who they are there to see. Then accompany them to that person's room or call the fellow student to meet their guest. If you feel suspicious or scared of the unknown person in any way, immediately contact either the RA or campus security.

- Keep first-floor windows closed and locked. This applies to dorm rooms, bathrooms, study and/or living rooms, and laundry rooms. If possible, install security bars and window jams for added security, but ensure they can be opened from the inside in the event you need an emergency escape.

- Attend campus programs designed to address the topic of security and keep updated on security matters and updates that may be posted in residence halls.

- Keep exterior doors closed at all times. Do not prop these doors open, as an open door invites nonresidents and other unauthorized intruders to enter your dorm.

General Security Tips for Students

- Students who share a room or suite should set ground rules at the start of the school year on how they will keep their room(s) and each other safe. When students respect their own and each other's property, obtaining buy-in and mutual agreement from all roommates is their best defense against crime.

- Do not leave computers or other valuables in vehicles or within shared living space, as they will disappear.

- Label, engrave, and take inventory of your property. Make a list of your belongings and retain that, along with information that identifies the property as belonging to you, in a safe place. Include serial numbers of computers and electronics, and photos of all your belongings. Note: Do not rely solely on your cell phone to retain this information. If your phone gets lost or stolen, your property tracking information disappears along with it.

- Do not walk around campus or your dorm wearing a headset or engrossed in texting, games, or talking on your phone. Remain alert in all environments at all times.

- Understand how the school communicates with students in the event of an emergency. Do they send a blast email or text message to all students? Do they post news and updates on the school's website? Do they post news and updates on electronic signs located strategically around campus?

- Protect your personally identifiable information on social media. Don't reference your dorm or campus location, or post photos that show where you might be at a given time. Postings such as these alert would-be criminals to the fact your room is empty as well as your own whereabouts on campus. The general Internet community does not need to know this information.

- If you are ever the victim of a crime or receive threats or obscene or harassing phone calls, text messages, or emails, report the incident to campus security immediately. Do not ignore the issue, as your action can protect you and others from future harm.

Chapter 7: Mixed-Use Properties

A mixed-use property is one that includes both residential and commercial, institutional, or industrial space. Examples of multiuse, multipurpose buildings could be a small, three-story storefront building that has two apartments on the third floor, a doctor's office on the second floor, and a coffee shop at ground level. Many large apartment buildings integrate retail, cultural, or office space on lower levels with residences on the higher levels. A mixed-use development could be a single building, a complex of buildings, or an entire district or neighborhood that is designated as such. These buildings may have separate parking lots or underground garages.

More and more people are finding mixed-use properties desirable for the benefits they offer, with convenience, perhaps, being at the top of the list. For example, residents enjoy greater density of neighbors and the closeness of housing and businesses, and find these environments to be generally pedestrian and bicycle friendly. In some cases, residents own and operate their ground-floor business while living upstairs. Most residents will also feel safer in their upstairs apartment knowing that the ground-floor business is occupied during the day. In effect, both parties can become the eyes and ears for each other, in a unique version of a neighborhood business watch.

Property owners and managers of mixed-use facilities have more security issues to be concerned with than those of straightforward apartment or townhouse complexes. Property managers are responsible for the safety and well-being of not only the building's residents, but also of their business tenants, including staff, customers, and the public in general that are in the vicinity of the building. Depending on how the building is laid out, security could be handled by someone who serves as a type of concierge or by independent professionals hired to provide protection services to the people, the property, and the assets on property.

Get to know the retail owners and their hours of operations. Become familiar with their employees.

When thinking security for a multifamily mixed-use property, in addition to hiring a professional security company to guard and protect the building, property managers can take other very specific steps to ensure the entire property, not just the business on the ground floor, remains as safe as possible and all people and assets are fully protected. A breach in security for the business could mean a potential breach in security for the residents upstairs, and vice versa.

While nothing replaces the presence of an on-site security officer, especially during off or overnight hours, property managers who implement some or all of these steps, in particular those that add protection to the surrounding perimeter, may go a long way in deterring crime.

- Enhance and improve door security – Check with the insurance company to obtain door and lock standards, and comply with them.

- Implement keyless door entry, so the user needs a card or key fob to gain access to the building to better regulate who gains access to your facility.

- Install an alarm system – Should a burglar successfully break into your building or the business, a monitored, motion-activated alarm system will alert law enforcement and/or the business or property manager.

- Don't go completely dark when the building or business is closed. Install security lighting on the building exterior, in the parking lot/garage, and near entryways, and keep security lights on inside.

- Use security cameras and CCTV – Keep light sufficiently bright so images captured by your security cameras are plainly visible.

- Limit access to the roof and upper floors.

- Keep trees and shrubs a sufficient distance from the building so they cannot be used by a would-be intruder to gain access to a second-floor window.

- In addition to having well-lit entrances, place exterior lighting at an appropriate height, 12–14 feet off the ground, and direct the lighting appropriately for both interior and exterior patrols to have good visibility.

Today's criminals are more sophisticated than ever. Even though statistics show the majority of criminals gain entry through a window or door, in some cases, they have figured out how to bypass existing security systems, and enter properties through unconventional means, such as from the roof, through the HVAC system, or via an adjacent building.

Questions for you to consider when you are deciding the best security strategy for your mixed-use property:

- How does the tenant and business diversity change the ongoing needs of the location?
- Do any trends or neighboring property concerns or activities exist that would cause tenants to leave?

Chapter 8: Why Hire a Professional Security Company?

Security guards and officers should be an integral component of any residential community's security program. Even when communities are designed and built to optimize natural and structural security and when property managers of those same communities employ only state-of-the-art security technology, one important element is still missing—the human element. Human security officers employ skills no full-scale automated security plan can—observation, training, familiarity, and judgment—all necessary to control and contribute to proper and appropriate people and property protection.

Every security strategy needs both depth and breadth if it is to be fully effective. Security must be deployed in layers, with every layer in the security plan adding substance and value. In other words, every layer in the plan matters. Highly visible security vehicles and professional security officers are key components in a layered plan, and also the strongest deterrents to crime. The below figure, discussed in depth in Chapter 2, depicts the layers of a residential community, and signals where security measures may need to be taken.

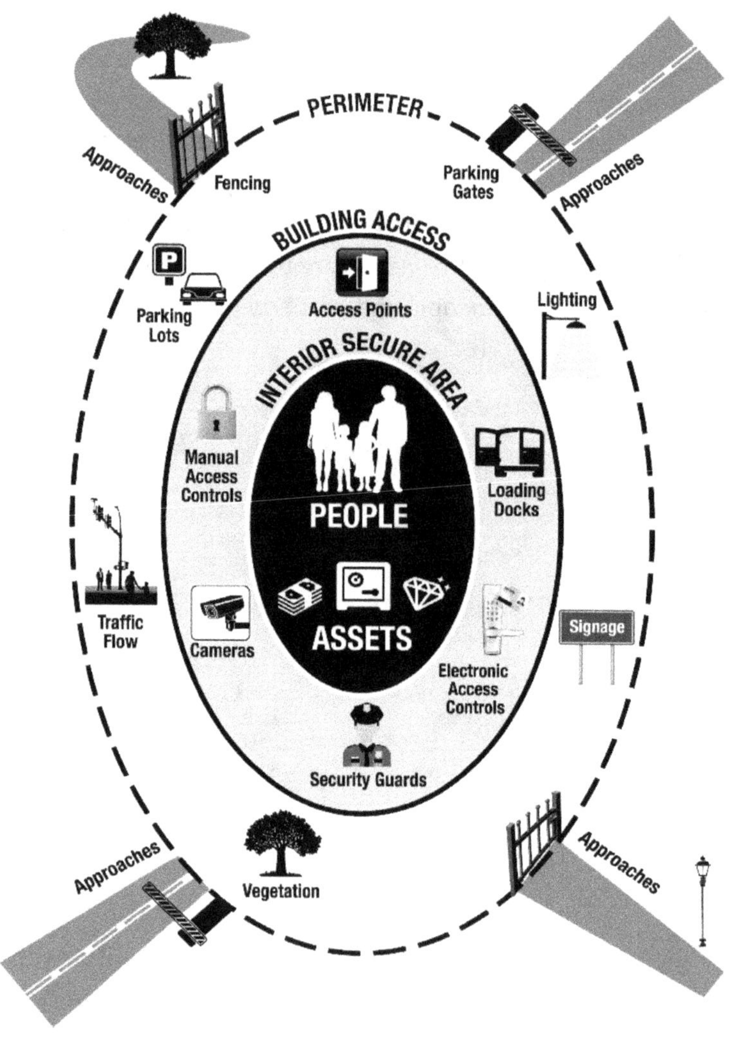

A professional (human) security company provides two additional qualities of high value. One is speed of response; when immediate action is called for, this type of rapid response is preprogrammed into the mindset of a security professional. The second quality is peace of mind. The presence of professional officers puts residents at ease and assures property managers and owners their property is being cared for.

Cost is a major factor when deciding to use a professional security company. A balance must be struck between ensuring adequate levels of physical protection are provided and what that protection costs. Too much security means you spend money unnecessarily on the security company when those funds could be applied toward additional security measures a community needs, such as additional lighting. The flip side is spending too little money on a security force and, for example, bringing in a guard for overnight hours only. With no daytime coverage, the community remains vulnerable from dawn to dusk. The larger sense of safety and assurances of security really have no price tag, but their perceived value to residents and property owners and managers is enormous.

Look at just a few of the ways the human element affords additional layers of protection:

- Vehicle access controls – To check vehicle and driver identification, inspect vehicles for irregularities, and address discrepancies appropriately
- Alarm situation assessment – To determine if an intrusion actually occurred or if an alarm was false
- Easily and readily mobile – Officers patrol communities on foot and in vehicles, observing the vicinity and noting irregularities to report or further investigate

Decision Made

Congratulations! You've decided to hire a professional security firm to provide guard and patrol services to secure the people and property of the multifamily community you manage. Your next step should be to compare and contrast the different companies you will be considering for hire. When you receive strong, effective security services, you and your tenants and residents may rest easy and feel safe and secure both at home and anywhere else on property.

Not All Security Companies Are Created Equal

Your research for the right security company for your community should keep a variety of factors in mind so you can be certain you will be receiving the most effective security services for your property. The minimum expectations detailed below provide a foundation for starting your search for the best company to meet your requirements. If any security company you research cannot agree to these expectations, you would do well to move on to another more responsive company.

- Training – Security guards and officers should receive both in-classroom and onsite training that can be verified. Training should be applicable to the post or posts to be filled, and should include all relevant policies and procedures. Training should include observation and challenge techniques, investigations, patrol procedures, report writing, emergency medical assistance and first aid, and security equipment operation.

- Patrols – Frequent patrols, both on foot and in marked vehicles, keep security guards alert and aware, which means they perform their job more effectively. Patrols also mean your property receives the necessary amount of surveillance and provides the presence your tenants/residents should expect.

- Communications – Proper, timely, effective communications between security staff and the landlord, property management company, or homeowners' association enhance guard services. Communications should be in the form of email, direct phone call, or text message, and a member of the security staff should be available 24/7 to take calls from them and from residents.

- Security supervisor presence and availability – Your security guard services will be optimized by the availability of an on-duty supervisor who oversees all guard activity and makes random site visits to make sure the guard(s) is doing his/her job.

- Security team familiarity—Know those who will be on duty day and night to protect your property and residents, including their supervisor/manager. When you know them and they know you, that is, when you have an established business relationship, the effectiveness of the services they provide increases.

- Professionalism - At all times, security officers and supervisors should adhere to a standard of ethics and code of conduct.

Dig Deeper When You Want the Best

We've all heard the term *rent-a-cop*. Merriam-Webster defines the term, often used disparagingly, as a security worker (a guard) who is not a police officer. Comments posted by readers online where the dictionary's definition appears may add to the negative perception: "... a college security vehicle... [had] two rent-a-cops in it. They were slumped down low in their seats and looked aimless and bored." Or this explanation: "... someone impersonating a cop." Then, in defense, one commenter said the term rent-a-cop is "... a derogatory phrase misrepresentative of today's security officers that are comparable to off-duty police officers, some with nearly as much training and expertise." Clearly Merriam-Webster could go further in their definition, and they probably would if they were fully informed on what goes into making a top-notch private security company.

The right combination of people, processes, and technology is the necessary foundation behind any first-rate security company.[25] Property managers and homeowner associations should keep this combination in mind when seeking out a potential security firm.

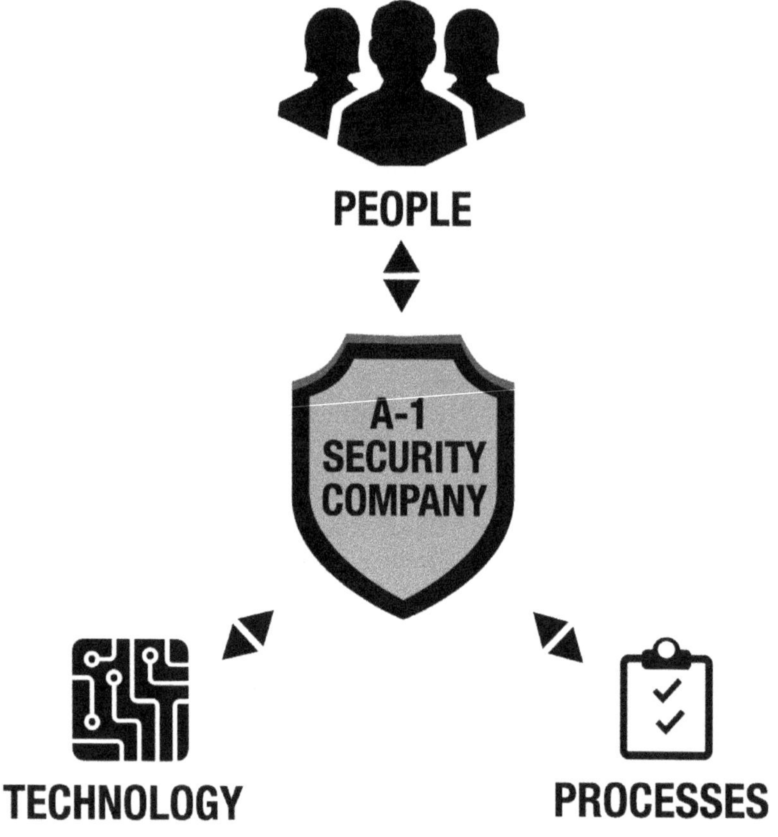

[25] Blog: The Best Security Company: What Does It Mean? by Courtney Sparkman, as posted on http://www.officerreports.com/blog/the-best-security-company/

Consider the people a security company employs. The bulk of them will be officers and/or guards. A top-notch company knows how to find—and keep—good officers. With the right personnel in terms of training and work ethic, security officer turnover decreases, and customer satisfaction increases.

When you have answers to the following questions, your job of evaluating a security company and the people they employ becomes easy.

- How does the security company screen candidates?
- How does the company recruit its officers? Do they tap into a broad, diverse pool of applicants so that they may find the best?
- What steps does the company take in its hiring process? For example, is there an onboarding step where new employees are taught the company's standards and expectations?
- What training do officers receive both as routine and on-site at a client location?
- What company benefits do officers receive? Do officers have the potential to develop themselves and advance? Is there an employee recognition program?
- What are the qualifications of the company management and executives? Do the managers directly responsible for managing client relationships have adequate skills and training for that aspect of their job?

Another people factor to evaluate is the responsiveness of company management. How responsive are they to client questions and concerns? Do they show they truly care about their clients? Are security guard supervisors open to frequent communication with property managers, landlords, and school officials? A good security company understands how critically important it is to keep the lines of communication open—a step that lets clients know they matter.

Next, consider the security company's processes. A good company will have a multitude of processes and procedures, but not all of them will be relevant for every client. Management should have no concern delineating the processes they will follow when it comes to patrolling and protecting your specific property. Also important is to know the company tracks process quality and effectiveness. For example, does the company preplan and test each process to know every quality requirement will be met? What is the process for management/client communication? Will there be regular meetings between the two? How will the company handle supervisor site visits, both scheduled and random? Does the company prepare daily client-specific/client-requested post orders for the security team to follow? Lastly, what indicators does the company measure (metrics) and how do they define success?

Technology can—and should—play a big role in the provisioning of security services. First, how do security officers check in for duty when they arrive on site? How does the security company track each officer's tour as they make their rounds during patrols? Do they use GPS or some other technology for that purpose? What other technology does the company use that makes an officer's job more effective? More efficient? How does the company manage the flow of information between the client and the security officers assigned to their property? What technology will the company provide for client use, for example, for incident reporting and tracking?

Beyond the people, processes, and technology, other considerations to keep in mind when evaluating the productivity and effectiveness of any professional security guard firm include:

- How much collaboration exists between the security company and local/state/federal law enforcement?
- Do residents know how to contact security when needed?

- Will the company provide a copy of their guard company license and evidence of insurance coverage?

- Do officers always provide detailed written activity logs following each patrol?

- Does the company allow clients to be named as an "additionally insured" on their policy and indemnify them from their negligent acts?

- How does the security company address performance concerns or inappropriate behavior on the part of their officers?

Just as every property is different, every security company is different. A top-notch security firm will listen to, and work closely with, property managers, landlords, and homeowners' associations to customize a security program to meet their very specific needs.

> *We recently helped a large client with a very unique issue... The client called us on Memorial Day requesting an immediate solution for a brand-new property. They needed it quickly, and it had to be an all-in solution. We spent the rest of the holiday developing a plan, and traveled to meet the client the next day to present the solution. The client agreed to it halfway through. We assembled vendors who provided temporary fencing and signage around the property; covered the pool; handled monthly landscaping; installed temporary lighting in low-lit areas; conducted 24/7 security patrols; developed an access control plan, video monitoring, and traffic barricades; and placed a security manager on site. We continue to conduct operations on this property, and this work has propelled our brand in the market. In addition, we received business from six more of their properties.*

Additional questions for you to consider when you are selecting the best security company for your community:

- What solutions for security have you already invested in?
- How do you measure the results of previous investments?
- What value or return on investment are you receiving?
- How can this value or return be improved?

Chapter 9: Why Signal 88 Security?

"We're here."

Signal 88 Security believes safety is a basic human right and need. Simply put, our mission is to provide peace of mind through security—a mission that defines our behavior and drives our actions every single day.

At Signal 88 Security, we are both called to serve and devoted to service. This calling is at the core of every person who wears our uniform. We build our name and reputation on our ethics of humility and decency and on living the essential humanity of the Golden Rule.

We believe the people we serve will never forget how we made them feel. At all times, we are conscious of the trust, responsibility, and accountability our clients place in us. We hope our tagline of "We're here" brings them peace of mind. To further reflect that sentiment, we refer to our employees as *officers*, not *guards*. The word *officer* connotes professionalism and conveys an elevated sense of the services we provide, which ultimately gives those we protect an added sense of security.

Through the character of our employees and leaders, we acquire, retain, and manage the trust of our customers. Skill and competence at what we do, seamless communication, and total alignment with our values make it happen. Through simplicity, professionalism, value, and quality, we solve today's increasingly complex security needs. A corporate client dealing with a threat of workplace violence said simply, "It's good to know that you are out there." Another said, "I can sleep better at night knowing that you and your team are watching over us."

To help meet the need we all have to feel safe, Signal 88 Security provides a full suite of world-class, industry-leading security services for residential, commercial, retail, and institutional customers. Our security solutions are custom designed to provide the exact level of protection our clients require. From roving vehicle patrols to dedicated services to security consultations, we can say with full confidence that our clients receive security and protection services from the best in the industry.

Our Beliefs

- The courage of conscious leadership – We are here as leaders, and believe in doing what is right, leading by example, and assuming the responsibility and accountability that comes with this duty.

- **The pioneering footprint** – We look at both the ground in front of us and the horizon in the distance, and employ distinguishing qualities of investigation, exploration, and discovery to reach our destination.

- **The journey to peace of mind** – We understand peace of mind is built upon the twin pillars of safety and security, and strive daily to make sure our customers find this feeling through delivery of our promise.

- **The humility of decency** – We serve others through what we do and how we do it, honored to help others achieve their goals with our commitment to the greater good and positive social impact.

- **The ethic of opportunity** – We create opportunity for others to align with the beliefs and values that anchor our conduct so they may create a future of meaningful importance and wealth creation.

Our Mission and Core Values

At Signal 88 Security, our mission is to provide peace of mind so you can pursue your passion in life. In everything we do, we operate according to five core values, a fundamental code of conduct in which we believe. These core values help us meet the challenges and questions we face daily, and facilitate how we solve problems and coach others for the good of all. In essence, these core values define how we do business.

- We drive with passion in everything we do because passion connects people to purpose.

- We live in integrity and honesty because without these our company and our brand would be hollow.

- We build and maintain relationships with others because healthy success can only be created out of mutual respect.

- We serve our communities without hesitation because serving is the active ingredient in service.

- We learn something every day by holding an open-minded approach to everything we do.

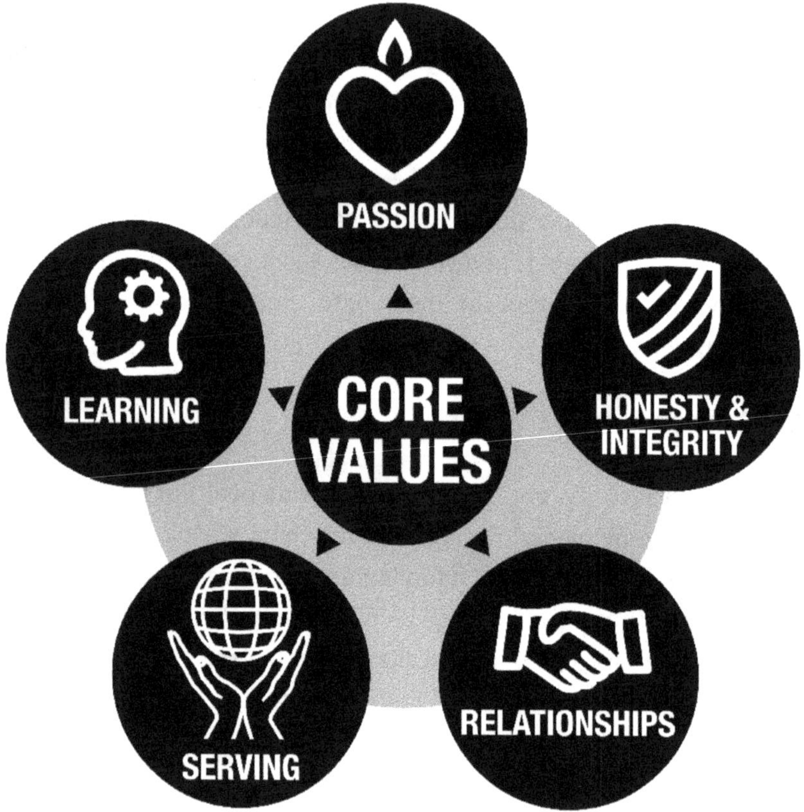

When we serve the community with integrity, when we demonstrate passion—and compassion—during difficult times, we build valuable connections and relationships. We also build our business and further strengthen the Signal 88 Security brand and reputation.

I got a hug and a thank you from one client simply because we called 911 when we observed a fire on the property and stayed to help. The client was so pleased they signed with us for six additional properties.

Our Services

Signal 88 Security offers a variety of security services to meet every need. In collaboration with our clients, we customize our security program around their requirements. We offer the following:

- Community-based dedicated security with highly visible officers who deter crime and provide a sustained presence in multifamily residential communities

- Vehicle patrols, our flagship service, with random patrols in well-marked vehicles that provide visual deterrence

- Emergency response to security alarms, to decrease the likelihood of theft, burglary, property damage, or some other loss

- Door checks to ensure entrances and exits are properly secured to limit or prevent after-hours access

- Pool lockups to prevent entry into a pool area outside of posted pool hours

- Event security with uniformed officers onsite for event attendees and organizers

Technology in Security

Technology plays an important and valuable role in how Signal 88 Security provisions its services. We use a proprietary, state-of-the-art suite of security technology designed to maximize employee resources and time and increase the effectiveness and efficiency of our operations.

Our user-friendly online client portal—accessible on any mobile or desktop device—allows clients to see their Signal 88 Security officer schedule, so clients know exactly who is working, and when. Through the portal, clients have access to all videos, photos, and reports filed on their behalf in the normal course of business we conduct on their property. And client invoicing and payment is also handled conveniently through the online portal.

Just as we use technology to facilitate our clients' ability to track their security-related services, we employ cutting edge technology for our officers to perform their duties as safely, capably, and effectively as possible. Through web-enabled Android and Apple cell phone and tablet devices, our officers access the company systems and apps they use in the course of carrying out their duties. The most common tools available to them include:

- Web and mobile accessibility through the 88Edge App - Officers log in and use a mobile app for almost everything they do: checking schedules and messaging management; clocking in and out; tracking training and certifications; checking client post orders that tell them specifically what needs to be done at every client location, how to do it, who to contact under normal conditions, for maintenance issues, and for emergencies. The 88Edge App is an officer's lifeline to everything he or she does.

- Post orders management – Post orders provide instructions for handling a variety of situations an officer may encounter at a client's site. They include pictures, maps, and/or typed orders. Post orders are updated as new policies are applied to the site or officers take on new roles at the site. Officers are required to acknowledge receipt and understanding of all post orders and prompted to check post orders whenever a change occurs.

- GPS tracking and attendance – Our global positioning system lets us know exactly where officers are at all times. The system periodically pings an accompanying device to collect an officer's current GPS coordinates and updates the location accordingly.

- Geofencing – Geofencing uses the GPS in our mobile devices to track an officer's positioning in reference to defined geographical boundaries. Using this virtual barrier, we track officer location and provide real-time notifications as they enter or exit the defined geographical boundaries.

- Maintenance and incident reports – We arrange client-requested reporting categories and subcategories for reporting incidents at their location. Each incident category, such as Maintenance, can have a distinct notification, so the user can view the reports most relevant to him or her. Reports can be set for any required category and provided to specific individuals or groups.

- Randomized patrol routing – By varying patrol routes on a random basis, potential criminals will be unable to predict when or where a patrol will occur.

- Real-time alerts – Officers receive immediate notification via their device. A broadcast message option—commonly used to alert officers to adverse weather conditions, Amber alerts, and developing situations on properties—is available to send mass messages to active field officers.

- Message with Siren - A text message can be sent to an officer through 88Edge with a siren sound that overrides the volume set on the officer's device. This ensures the officer hears the tone.

- Remote speak message – This service speaks messages to the officer. Text submitted in the message window is read aloud to the officer through the speaker on their device.

- Remote audio and video recording - Our cell phone and tablet devices pick up sound (audio) via their microphone and video via their camera. Once the device has captured a clip, a recording is sent to our cloud servers, and property managers can view them instantly on their Live Dashboard via the 88Edge Web Portal.

- Daily activity reporting and tracking – Automated functions let officers enter reports efficiently and with minimal human error. We can track and report on anything clients need watched. We can take pictures and video, and answer literally any question they might have every time we go to their site. We can track and document the temperature of a room or a reading from a gauge, from initial tracking to automatically reporting and plotting the information on charts and reports for clients. Reports, videos, and pictures are all available online and can be delivered automatically to the client daily, weekly, and anytime the client wants. All information is completely searchable and reportable online and downloadable into PDF, CSV, and Excel formats.

- Resident database management – Officers can track all resident activity to know who is on property in cases of emergencies or other needs. We can scan driver's licenses or IDs and compare that information and pictures with what property management has provided us from their property management systems.

- Visitor tracking – Officers track all visitor activity, including pre-approved visitors, via an online database. 88Edge can keep a list, by resident, of preapproved visitors who are permitted access. We can also track banned-and-barred people to make sure they are not given access. Our system allows us to scan and log licenses, photos, and signatures, and also print out visitor badges if required.

- Package tracking – We scan packages when they arrive from a delivery company and send an automated email to alert the resident that a package has been delivered for them. The resident picks up the package and signs for it to complete the tracking record.

- Dispatch center – We track and respond to inbound calls and/or other client communications immediately, and deploy security services as needed. Our dispatch center is a robust system that uses different components to manage, assign, and complete jobs. Workflows identify the different stages a ticket can pass through, from job creation through completion, with a roadmap that connects the different stages and statuses along the way. Dispatch report forms are used to create field reports to be completed in collaboration by both the dispatcher and the officer, with each completing their assigned fields in the reports. Put simply, the dispatcher provides information to the officer so the officer understands the purpose of the job. The officer completes the work and sends requisite information back to the dispatcher to confirm the job has been completed. A final dispatch form is a compilation of the information provided by the officer and dispatcher.

- Support tickets – These manage and maintain all vital information for every issue reported, tracked, and closed out.

- CCTV integration – Closed-circuit television integration provides video surveillance of doors and alarms to detect intruders, monitor alarm status, and more, with video feeds sent directly to officers. Property coverage is increased by giving officers access to multiple feeds from any browser and adding one or multiple camera feeds or by managing multiple sites from the same dashboard.

- Employee safety features provide added peace of mind and safety in hazardous situations – 88Edge's Solitary Officer Protection System ensures we comply with labor and safety regulations, while also lowering risk and liability. Officers receive automatic notifications when they need to check in, and real-time notifications keep management informed of an officer's inactivity.

- Franchise knowledge resources – Signal88 Security's franchise group provides and maintains an extensive intranet site: *SOAP* – Sales, Operations, Administration, and Promise. In the Promise section, for example, franchise owners find leadership and mentoring training and support, annual convention information, and a gamut of marketing resources.

Employee Training and Development

We learn something every day by holding an open-minded approach to everything we do.

Learning is one of Signal 88 Security's five core values. Well-trained employees grow and develop with the confidence, competence, and life behaviors they need to succeed personally and professionally, and to be a hero, mentor, cheerleader, and expert in their field.

CEO Reed Nyffeler greets and welcomes all new employees to Signal 88 Security via a video on our interactive 88University online classroom. New-employee orientation introduces employees to the Signal 88 Security way of doing business. They learn *how* we do business by taking e-learning courses aligned with their specific role. Coursework and training topics include fully detailed security training, report-writing, customer service, client-specific security requirements, leadership, life skills, and more. In addition, officers receive training in the field on all tactical and security-related competencies relating to their role and client assignment and also complete training in compliance with applicable state and local laws and regulations.

We even take steps to review studies and the psychology behind mental health disorders and psychological distress and their connection to perceived safe or unsafe neighborhoods to learn what steps we can take to improve people's very real living situations.

The depth and breadth of training our employees receive ensure they are fully qualified and capable of addressing whatever security issue falls within their scope of responsibilities.

Below we provide detail on a sampling of our employee trainings.

- Top 10 De-escalation Tips (as outlined by Crisis Prevention Institute) – This includes an explanation of why each tip is important and recommended steps an officer should (or should not) take to successfully defuse a situation

- What to do when police and/or emergency vehicles are on a property where our officers are assigned

- Step-by-step procedures for handling alarm calls – Most often these are noise-related or involve people loitering on property

- Procedures for handling people who are loitering on property
- How to handle a situation involving an unlocked door
- Procedures for vehicle break-in – including both if the officer observed the break-in or came across it after the break-in occurred
- Procedures for implementing a ban-and-bar status to remove a person from a location either temporarily or permanently – This includes working with local police and a Signal 88 Security manager to complete all necessary steps
- Steps to take to assess community lighting
- Procedure for when drugs are suspected on property

Report Writing

Thorough, detailed client reports are the primary indicator of the excellent job Signal 88 Security officers do every day and every night. Our reporting process is one of the key benefits we offer our clients. The reports we provide contain our observations from every patrol—vehicle or foot—that we perform. Through these detailed reports property managers know we are doing our job and also working hard to keep the communities we protect free from vandalism and theft.

Well-written reports demonstrate to property managers and landlords that we are diligent in carrying out our job. In fact, every report produced contains an entry that describes in detail some site-specific observation or event that is unique to the time and place an officer was on duty. For example, beyond an officer's simple report indicating he or she completed a scheduled foot or vehicle patrol, the officer also diligently documents other observations made while on patrol, such as lighting that is not functioning or foot or vehicle traffic seen in the area at the time.

Because we want each report to contain all the information a client would need to be fully informed, we train our officers to write a report based on the "5 W's and 1 H": Who is the report about? What happened? Where did the event take place? When did it happen? Why did it happen? How did it happen?

We train our officers to provide a daily status report on those items that are most important to property managers. These include:

- Gates (if the community has them) – Property managers rely on their gates and spend a lot of money to keep them in working order. A status on gates should appear in each report.

- Fencing and perimeter – Property managers are always interested in knowing details of any perimeter assessment an officer makes, especially of those areas not visible from the road.

- Courtyards and common areas - Our report includes what the officer saw, heard, or looked for and found as a result of the patrol of courtyards and common areas.

- Mail, laundry, fitness room areas - These areas should remain well-lit and handicapped accessible. We report on these areas whether they are lit and accessible or if a vehicle or obstruction is present. Our report includes the condition of these areas, including if they are open or closed, the lights are on or off, the area is occupied or unoccupied.

- Office, clubhouse, and maintenance buildings – Reports include detail indicating both when doors are locked and when the officer encounters one that is not locked.

- Lighting – We know that adequate lighting is the first line of defense after the sun goes down. Reports include detail on perimeter lighting as well as interior and courtyard lights.

Occasionally, property managers ask us to pay particular attention to a particular area or activity. We check and document our observations of the area or activity multiple times throughout each shift.

Our officers are expected to watch and report on road hazards and obstructions and on road conditions during inclement weather. Officers will also look for, and note, flooding and pipes that may have broken and burst during stretches of extreme cold, storm damage anywhere on property due to high winds, and graffiti.

Property managers and landlords are also very interested in knowing about the people we encounter on their property. They know who lives in the community they manage, so our reports detail the person's name and/or apartment number where we observe activity. Our officers know that one of the most important things we can do to control a property is to stop and challenge pedestrian presence. As mundane as these encounters may be, we understand the property manager's desire to know who is coming and going onsite, and so report on these as well.

When you hire Signal 88 Security, you can rest assured we are present on the job as scheduled and dedicated to adhering to client instructions, as demonstrated by our reports.

Sample Reports

What follows are four examples of actual Signal 88 Security officer reports, with identifying information redacted. Property owners want to see detail on what matters most to them, and we deliver.

Alarm Report – Noise Complaint
Reported at: XXX (location)
Date/time: Sep 12th 01XX until Sep 12th 01XX

I received an alarm call from an anonymous resident of 10025 XXX XXX, building 25. They refused to give any information on their name or number. They said there were loud noises coming from one of the rooms. They were not sure which room it was coming from. I arrived on the property soon after. I foot patrolled through all floors of building 25. I stopped in front of apartment #4, and could hear people shouting and talking very loudly. I knocked on the door and was greeted by gentleman named XXX; he was the resident. I informed him that they needed to keep their voices down. He apologized to me, and went inside to tell them to keep it quiet. I observed inside the apartment a few other guests, and a couple bottles of alcohol. At this time, they were being very respectful and compliant. I waited outside of apartment #4 for several minutes and everything remained quiet. No further action was taken.

Vehicle/Foot Patrol – Asked to leave...
Reported at: XXX (location)
Date/time: Apr 22nd 15XX until Apr 22nd 15XX

I arrived on site and began a vehicle patrol of the property. Due to the heavy rain, I focused on the exterior hallways. By unit 5624, three teenage males were on the top of the stairs. When I drove by and pulled into a parking space, the three males exited the hallway and headed towards the edge of the building by unit 5648. I observed a fourth teenager pass me on the hallway and I asked if he lived on site. He stated he did and that he could not remember the unit. When I saw him head towards the other teenagers, I entered the main door to the units and saw the teenagers entering unit 5648. I then continued on my patrol where I observed three teenagers again, minus the fourth, in an exterior hallway between units 5729 and 5723. The three saw me and headed out where the maintenance worker saw the three as well. All three ran out along the west plaza towards school entrance. The maintenance worker showed me two broken doors into the laundry room of that building. I continued my vehicle patrol up to unit 14862 and looked behind the garages by the tree and resident's porch. There were no teenagers and the whole area was covered in mud and puddles. I did not see the teenagers again. There was no other unusual activity.

Vehicle Patrol – Trespasser (banned and barred individual)
Reported at: XXX (location)
Date/time: Jan 29th 15XX until Jan 29th 16XX

I arrived on site, turned on the LED lights, and began a vehicle patrol. When I pulled up to XXX Court and U plaza I encountered several groups of teenagers totaling around 25-30. As I pulled up, one ran and tried to kick the air but his shoe fell off. The rest mainly scattered. I followed around and pointed towards a small group that had branched off to walk down behind the townhomes. I pointed several times to them to move out of the yards. I was pulled aside by a young male teenager who lives in unit 5748. He stated that a banned teenager named Steven was in unit 5747. I pulled off in front of the unit 5748 and a male teenager, who stated that he was the other teenager's brother, asked if there were any concerns or issues as the teenager who hangs out across the street had been picking on his brother. I stated there were not any issues right now. I headed to the leasing office and spoke with a female leasing agent who called and confirmed there was a Steven at unit 5747 at this time. I informed her I will check our record to find a last name for Steven. No further action was wanted per client request.

Alarm Response – Fire Alarm
Reported at: XXX (location)
Date/time: May 29th 20XX until May 29th 21XX

The team received an alarm call from Alex XXX (***-***-****) regarding a smoke detector going off inside the clubhouse. I directly contacted Alex to gather more information regarding the smoke detectors. He informed me that the fire department was en route and wanted me to check it out as well. Upon my arrival to the property I did not see any fire trucks yet. I accessed the front double doors and could right away hear the alarm system buzzing, but did not smell smoke. I noticed the alarm panel read "basement alert." I patrolled down to the basement and did not see/smell any indication of a possible fire. I did notice a water leak coming from the frame of the door leading into the kitchen area of the basement. I contacted Alex back to inform him of the situation. Upon my departure, I silenced the alarm and then reactivated it. After finishing my report in the parking lot, a gentleman named Mark XXX, who was with XXX Real Estate, approached me. While I was filling Mark in on the situation, another gentleman from XXX Alarm Systems approached me. He requested that I show him what I observed when I arrived and how I turned off the system. As he was trying to figure out how the system was tripped, I encountered leaks throughout the building, which was caused from a plugged gutter. Mark authorized me to leave at this time. No further activity to report on at this time.

Client Training

Signal 88 Security possesses extensive expertise on a wide range of security-related topics. Because we understand how important it is for people to feel secure where they live, work, and play, we make ourselves available to provide training in virtually any location and in any format—on-site, webinars, articles for publication, blogs, etc.

We will meet with property owners and managers, homeowner associations and boards, building managers and landlords. We are also available to meet with attorneys for any of the above who need to protect themselves against residents who, in our litigious society, are quick to threaten lawsuit action.

The safety and security topics we routinely address in our training presentations generally fit into two categories: 1) tips for a more secure environment and 2) information for professional security companies. At Signal 88 Security, we are flexible in how we provide our training and can combine or break out topics depending on individual client needs. Below is a list of the most commonly requested training topics.

Topics on Tips for a More Secure Environment

- Security audit/assessment
- Safety and security policy
- Safety committee
- Safety column in newsletter
- Partners – law enforcement, neighbors, community groups
- Pet policies and enforcement made easy
- Shared building access guides
- Car safety

- Parking – what to do, how to enforce the rules
- Crimeproof your home
- Home safety/avoiding property theft
- Cameras and monitoring – guides, to do's, use policy
- Resident's criminal record – HOA requirements?
- Holiday home safety
- Leveraging technology
- How to address trespassers, salespeople, political canvassers, vagrants

Additional questions for you to keep in mind when considering Signal 88 Security to fulfill your security needs:

- How do you see diverse cultures affecting the services provided by your security vendor?
- What results do you believe technology will provide as you affirm the value of a particular security company?
- What is the application of the information provided by a security company worth? What is its value?

Chapter 10: A Day in the Life of Signal 88 Security Heroes

I have helped customers many times over the years, but as a Signal 88 franchise owner, my help seems minor compared to the times our team members have helped others.

We at Signal 88 Security believe our employees are heroes, in that their life's goal is to care humbly for those in their community and those they love by providing security and building a personal, local, and meaningful brand in the process. Our heroes have the passion to create peace of mind because they truly love what they do and they are good at it. The Signal 88 Security core beliefs and values shape the company, its owners, and every employee in our daily promise and delivery on our commitment to serving others and living the Golden Rule. Our desire is to serve others and succeed in life in the process. The anecdotes and quotes that follow are representative of the company philosophy across the country.

I truly enjoy making a positive impact on other people's lives. The security industry is not the most glamorous, but when you create a relationship with a client that gives them peace of mind knowing we're looking out for their assets day and night, it gives a huge sense of pride for everyone involved.

The president of one Signal 88 Security franchise tells the following story:

> *One of our guards, an immigrant, just bought a house. I bought a "starter" tool kit and a hundred-dollar gift card for him as a house-warming present—just as you would with anyone. Then I started thinking about his situation and it hit me. This guy immigrates to America, gets a job as a security guard, and is able to buy a house. He's living the American dream right in front of us and no one will notice. He's a good officer and does his job well. His reports are a little lacking because English is his second language, but he's getting better. He is never late to work and always has a great attitude. So, here we have someone who moves here from some war-torn country in the Middle East, gets a job with Signal 88, and buys a house. How awesome is that? How do we recognize that?*

Signal 88 Security heroes go above and beyond, and do what is needed to ensure the safety and security of all involved.

> *One of my officers found a toddler wandering around a community by herself and stayed with her until her parents were located.*

Another Signal 88 Security franchise owner tells the story of how he helped a business customer.

> *The chairperson of a county business organization requested emergency security coverage due to a perceived threat from a male member of the organization. This member demonstrated clear behavioral health issues. The*

> *chairperson and larger group observed his atypical behaviors and felt threatened. We went out immediately and put plainclothes officers on property for a week and a half. These officers were the best of the best—highly trained in this type of issue and carrying a concealed weapon. In addition, we provided a one-hour training program on workplace violence and developed a response plan in case anything occurred. The organization wanted to remove this man from their membership, but their process required them to identify cause and schedule a hearing. Fortunately, this person saw the evidence against him and resigned voluntarily.*

After this incident, the client provided the following testimonial:

> *Our organization encountered an unexpected need for heightened security, and Signal 88 Security responded quickly in organizing a team of professionals to help. Specifically, the owner of the company put everyone's concerns at ease with his background in law enforcement and the manner in which he handled a stressful situation for us. The quality of the individuals that provided onsite protection for employees and the education they gave on how to respond to a threat was extremely helpful to our staff. We would not hesitate to hire Signal 88 Security again or recommend their services to other groups.*

This franchise owner is the first to tell you they were just doing their job, which goes to the company's tag line of "We're here." Our presence on-site provided an immediate de-escalation of the stress everyone in the workplace had been experiencing. They knew we were there to handle their problem and that they would not have to call 911.

Who Are These People?

The Signal 88 Security franchise network is owned and operated by people who care about providing peace of mind to the people in their local communities and who are deeply vested in fixing the broken or ineffective methods used by traditional security service providers for decades. The company owner intentionally injected technology into franchisee daily operations to produce a level of accountability previously unheard of in the industry. For example, through the integration of proprietary software, owners have real-time access to vital property information and highly effective service offerings engineered to deter criminal activity.

They know that every new day brings a new challenge, and they are ready and well prepared to step up to it. Our leaders enjoy their role and also the strategic planning aspect of running their own business, from helping employees grow in their chosen career to growing the company through market acquisition.

Franchise owners are, however, more than just savvy business people. Yes, knowing how to run a business adds to each franchisee's success. Beyond that, owners bring a wealth of life and professional experience as well. Many franchise owners have prior experience in the military and in local and federal law enforcement. They bring that experience and professionalism to running their own business—expertise that includes private security, strategic and tactical planning, tactical operations, security operations and management, emergency medical and fire response, and more.

Ask any Signal 88 Security franchise owner what keeps them up at night and they'll tell you it's their concern they will let someone on their team down, or that someone on their team or a client under their protection gets injured, or that their team will let down a client by not conducting their tasks properly. Customer and employee satisfaction and reputation in the community are top concerns.

> *When property and lives are protected, we fulfill our commitment to serve clients with intent and integrity.*

The "We're here" philosophy was once again on display when the following situation occurred:

A mentally ill person who had punched through a glass window was taken to the ER by ambulance. She had sustained a deep laceration of her arm and required treatment, but her demeanor was loud and threatening. In addition, she was covered in dried blood. The hospital staff requested that I respond and, along with the police, we were able to de-escalate her so she could be treated by the ER staff. Through our combined actions, we avoided further injury to this person and to the staff, and prevented blood borne exposures.

Individual franchise owners play a valuable role in the community. We own our security business for a reason—we love what we do and believe in supporting our communities and the people who live, work, and play in them. Our job is to provide security services, yes, but beyond that, building relationships and earning the trust and friendship of those we serve is what we value most—professionally and personally.

Additional questions for you to consider when you are thinking of using Signal 88 Security to fulfill your security needs:

- What perception does a poor security vendor employee create on your property?
- What difference can a committed, well-trained security employee—a Hero—make?

Signal 88 Security franchise owners are not in the business for the glory of it. Time and again, they say the simplest words and simplest expressions of gratitude from a customer are all the reward they need.

I never had a positive experience working with other security patrol companies before. By far, you are the best and have exceeded my expectations.

"Thank you. You guys are great."

Appendix

The pages that follow contain checklists of safety and security tips and recommendations for residents of multifamily communities and school/campus residence halls. Property managers, landlords, and school officials can provide these lists to homeowners, renters, and students as part of their ongoing security measures and also as new residents move into a property.

Security Tips for Apartment Renters

- Regardless of where you go on the property, inside or out, be consciously aware of your surroundings at all times. Remain alert and pay attention to specific areas of the building you live in: hallways, stairwells, storage rooms, laundry rooms, etc. Outside, be alert in parking and trash areas and common areas that include pools and sports and recreational facilities.

- Control your personal space inside the apartment—your bedroom—by establishing a barrier between you and any potential threat. For example, you can purchase a door stop that doubles as an alarm that goes off when an intruder enters. The cost for this easy type of security is approximately $10. Another type of barrier is a door pole that wedges into place from the floor to door handle. When you have these simple types of barriers in place, you have time to react appropriately, such as by calling the police or security company.

- Apartment roommates should set an agreement upfront regarding each other's guests. Do you trust who he or she brings into the apartment? Respect each other's wishes regarding who is permitted to stay overnight or remain in the apartment while their host is not present. Statistics show that the overwhelming majority of attacks happen by someone the victim knows.

- Set ground rules when multiple roommates move in together on how they will keep their apartment and each other safe. Mutual respect for each other and each other's property should make obtaining buy-in easy. These types of agreements represent a best defense against crime.

General tips for security in an apartment environment:

- Call 911 and/or your building manager immediately to report suspicious behavior or activity.

- Get to know your neighbors and where they live. When you know the rightful residents, you can more easily spot a real intruder.

- As much as possible, use only well-lit sidewalks, doorways, hallways, and stairways. Report insufficient or malfunctioning lighting to your property manager for repair.

- Do not enter an elevator if you feel uncomfortable or are suspicious of another person on the elevator. Stand near the elevator control buttons and know which is the emergency button.

At home in your apartment:

- Before moving in, make sure the locks to your unit have been changed.

- Your main door should have a deadbolt lock and peephole so you can see who is outside your unit.

- If your apartment does not already have a built-in security system, purchase a small security unit you can place on a door and set it to go off when there is an unauthorized entry.

- *Never* open your door to a stranger, no matter what they request. If necessary, call 911 or the property manager on the person's behalf, but do so from inside your locked apartment.

- List only your last name or first initial and last name on mailbox or intercom directory.

- Fit sliding glass doors and windows with appropriate auxiliary locking devices.

- First-floor and lower units should have additional security on the windows that prevent a burglar from raising the window and entering. A simple dowel placed vertically at one edge of the window does not allow the window to be opened. Just make sure you can easily remove the dowel yourself if you need to use the window as an escape route in the event of an emergency.

- Engrave and/or document a list of all items of value, and keep the list in a separate safe location.

When you go out, take precautions:

- Lock all doors and windows.

- When you return home, and something is amiss or you think someone is inside, don't go in. Call 911, Security, or the manager, and wait with a neighbor for help to arrive.

- At night, put TVs and lamps on a variety of timers set to go on and off at different times.

- Don't hide your spare key in what you think is your secret hiding place somewhere outside your unit; burglars are experts at finding people's secret hiding places. Let a trusted neighbor keep your spare key for you.

- Don't tempt burglars by leaving expensive or valuable items visible through windows or doors.

Checklist for the laundry room:

- Is the lighting in the laundry room bright and is the room clean and in good working order?

- If the laundry area is in a separate building, are the paths to the area clear, open, well lit, and visible?
- Is there a large mirror angled for residents who want to enter the laundry room to clearly see if anyone is inside before they enter?
- Is the laundry room door lockable from the inside? Does it include a proper panic bar/handle? Does the window on the door contain metal mesh to prevent someone from breaking the glass and unlocking the door from the outside?
- Consider doing laundry with a friend or neighbor (in pairs) – for safety in numbers.

Enjoy full use of your community's amenities:

- Are common areas, fitness/sporting areas, recreation areas, and the pool designated as for use only by residents and their invited guests?
- Do not go into common areas or recreational facilities if you are suspicious of one or more people already using the facility.
- Avoid areas where lighting is insufficient or malfunctioning; report the issue to the manager.
- Leave your jewelry, cash, wallet, and other valuables in your locked apartment.

Parking lots:

- Lighting in the parking lot should be bright; if lighting is deficient or faulty, report it to the manager.

- Park as close to your unit as possible, in a well-lit area.

- Parking spaces should not be identified with the same unit number/letter as the apartment or condo. This makes it hard for burglars to target units where they believe no one is home.

- Do not leave any items visible on the seats of your car or elsewhere. A burglar might think your $15 sunglasses are actually worth $200, and break in a window to steal them.

- Take advantage of all available car alarm devices and anti-theft technology.

- Whether your car is parked at your own apartment complex or elsewhere, always lock it and keep your keys in your possession.

Security Tips for Townhome and Condominium Homeowners

- Get to know, or at least recognize, other residents in your vicinity as well as other people who are regularly in your community, such as landscapers.

- When going away for an extended period of time, let a reliable, trustworthy neighbor know. If you are comfortable, leave your contact number and a copy of your house key with them, in case they need to reach you. Or, let them know if you plan on having someone check on your home while you are away. Stop newspaper and mail delivery so these items don't back up and provide a clue that no one is at home.

- Whether you're at work for the day or away for a week, don't let package deliveries sit on your front door step unattended. If possible, have packages delivered to a neighbor's address or plan deliveries to arrive at times you know you will be home.

- Set lights in different rooms on timers so they come on and go off at different times during evening and night hours. Along with that, hang window coverings that prevent people on the outside from looking in and seeing you and your belongings at night.

- Install multiple locks on doors and bolster the strength of existing locks. Lock sets, chains, and deadbolt locks make it more difficult for would-be thieves to break in. If your door doesn't have a peephole, install one and use it every time your doorbell rings.

- Keep valuables such as jewelry and electronics out of sight. By leaving them plainly visible, you invite thieves who will steal them and sell them immediately for cash.

- Engrave and/or document a list of all items of value, and keep the list in a separate safe location.

- The next best thing to having an interior alarm system is to install specialized theft-deterrent latches to windows and patio doors. These mechanisms do more than just keep windows locked. They let windows be open to a certain height, after which the mechanism blocks it from being opened further.

- Keep garage doors closed at all times when not in use to prevent thieves from stealing directly from your garage or gaining quick, easy entry to your home through the inside door.

- Install floodlights and/or motion-detection lighting on decks and patios and other areas or points of entry into your home or garage where general community lighting does not reach.

Security Tips for Homeowners in Age-Restricted Communities

- It is easy for some people to keep to themselves and not want to get involved in the goings-on in their community, but for everyone's safety and security, residents should get to know, or at least recognize, each other as well as other people who enter the community on a regular basis, such as landscapers.
- When traveling for an extended period, whether over a long weekend or three months over winter, let property management and a reliable, trustworthy neighbor know. If you are comfortable, leave your contact number and a copy of your house key with your neighbor, in case they need to enter your house or otherwise reach you. Or, if you plan on having someone else such as a family member check on your home while you are away, let your neighbor know.
- Stop newspaper and mail delivery so these items don't back up and provide a clue that no one is at home.
- Don't allow package deliveries to sit on your front door step unattended if you're away even for a day. If possible, have packages delivered to a neighbor's address or plan deliveries to arrive at times you know you will be home.
- Set lights on timers throughout your home so they come on and go off at different times during evening and night hours.
- Close blinds and drapes at night so people on the outside are unable to look in and see you or your belongings at night.
- Hire a locksmith to install multiple locks on doors and bolster the strength of existing locks. If you purchased the home on a resale, change the locks altogether. Lock sets, chains, and deadbolt locks make it more difficult for would-be thieves to break in.
- If your door doesn't have a peephole, install one and use it every time your doorbell rings.

- "Out of sight, out of mind." Valuables such as jewelry and electronics should be kept safely out of sight to avoid inviting thieves to break in and steal them.
- Engrave and/or document a list of all items of value, and keep the list in a separate safe location.
- Install specialized theft-deterrent latches on windows and patio doors. They are the next best thing to having an interior alarm system. Window lock mechanisms allow windows to open only to a certain height, after which the mechanism blocks it from being opened further.
- Unless you are pulling in or out of your garage, keep the garage door closed at all times. An open garage door is an open invitation to a thief to steal directly from your garage or gain quick, easy entry to your home through the inside door.
- Floodlights and/or motion-detection lighting installed on decks, patios, and other outside areas or points of entry into your home or garage provide additional lighting where general community lighting does not reach.

Security Tips for Students in On-Campus Residence Halls and Off-Campus Housing

- Familiarize yourself with the on-campus security company and know how to reach them from any location. Program the emergency phone number for campus security into your cell phone.

- Know who your Resident Advisor (RA) is as well as the location of the RA's room.

- Lock the door to your room when sleeping and anytime you leave, even if just to use the bathroom.

- Remain with your guests at all times. You are responsible for your guests and their actions. By escorting them, you not only track their actions, you let other students in the dorm know that your guest is authorized to be in the building.

- Do not let strangers into the building. Inform the unknown person he or she needs to call the person they are visiting, and that person will come to let them in. Or, ask the stranger who they have come to see and let that fellow student know they have a visitor waiting at the front door.

- If you see an unescorted person walking around the residence hall, approach and ask them who they are there to see. Then accompany them to that person's room or call the fellow student to meet their guest. If you feel suspicious or scared of the unknown person in any way, immediately contact either the RA or campus security.

- Keep first-floor windows closed and locked. This applies to dorm rooms, bathrooms, study and/or living rooms, and laundry rooms. If possible, install security bars and window jams for added security, but ensure they can be opened from the inside in the event you need an emergency escape.

- Attend campus programs designed to address the topic of security and keep updated on security matters and updates that may be posted in residence halls.

- Keep exterior doors closed at all times. Do not prop these doors open, as an open door invites nonresidents and other unauthorized intruders to enter your dorm.

General tips for students:

- Students who share a room or suite arrangement should set ground rules at the start of the school year on how they will keep their room(s) and each other safe. When students respect their own and each other's property, obtaining buy-in and mutual agreement from all roommates is their best defense against crime.

- Do not leave computers or other valuables in vehicles or within shared living space, as they will disappear.

- Label, engrave, and take inventory of your property. Make a list of your belongings and retain that, along with information that identifies the property as belonging to you, in a safe place. Include serial numbers of computers and electronics, and photos of all your belongings. Note: Do not rely solely on your cell phone to retain this information. If your phone gets lost or stolen, your property tracking information is gone along with it.

- Do not walk around campus or your dorm wearing a headset or engrossed in texting or games on your phone. Remain alert in all environments at all times.

- Understand how the school communicates with students in the event of an emergency. Do they send a blast email or text message to all students? Do they post news and updates on the school's website? Do they post news and updates on electronic signs located strategically around campus?

- Protect your personally identifiable information on social media and networks. Don't reference your dorm or campus location, or post photos that show where you might be at a given time. Postings such as these alert would-be criminals to the fact your room is empty as well as your own whereabouts on campus. The general Internet community does not need to know this information.

- If you are ever the victim of a crime, or if you ever receive threats or obscene and/or harassing phone calls, text messages, or emails, report the incident to campus security immediately. Do not ignore the issue, as your action can protect you and others from future harm.

Self-defense Tactics

Anyone can enhance their personal safety and reduce their chances of being attacked by learning and adhering to some common-sense self-defense strategies. When people know what to do or say and how to behave under certain circumstances, they effectively remove the target from their back and keep would-be attackers at bay.

Self-defense and security experts provide training and guidance on a variety of techniques to prevent assaults and help people protect themselves physically when they go out and conduct normal daily activities. The tips listed below are minimum steps to take to remain as safe as possible.

Avoid Dangerous Places and People

- Do not go in areas of high crime and steer clear of places where violent people (or those who may turn violent) gather.

Be Aware of Your Surroundings

- Familiarize yourself with who and what is normal in your day-to-day environment; rely on instinct when something/someone appears out of place.

De-escalate Verbal Conflicts

- Comply verbally to let the perpetrator win and maintain a dominant role; respond with one or more deflective statements and walk away.

Set Barriers/Create Distance

- Attackers hide around corners, between cars, and in recessed doorways—keep as much distance as possible between you and these potential threats.

Additional Resources

American Crime Prevention Institute: http://acpionline.com/.

Booth, Jamie, Stephanie L. Ayers, and Flavio F. Marsiglia (2012). "Perceived Neighborhood Safety and Psychological Distress: Exploring Protective Factors," *The Journal of Sociology & Social Welfare* 39 (4), Article 8. Retrieved from: http://scholarworks .wmich.edu/jssw/vol39/iss4/8.

Crime Analysis for Problem Solvers in 60 Small Steps: Use the problem analysis triangle. *Center for Problem-Oriented Policing*. Retrieved from http://www.popcenter.org/learning/60steps/ index.cfm?stepNum=8.

Felson, Marcus, and Mary Eckert (2016). *Crime and Everyday Life, Fifth Edition*. Los Angeles: Sage Publications.

Fennelly, Lawrence, J. (2013). *Effective Physical Security, Fourth Edition*. Waltham, MA: 2013.

Gore, Sheriff William D., *Apartment and Condominium Security*, San Diego County Sheriff's Department. Retrieved from https://www.sdsheriff.net/documents/apartment_condo.pdf.

Scott, David. (2014, September 30). Defense in depth and breadth: Securing the Internet of things [Web log post]. Retrieved from https://inform.tmforum.org/sponsored-feature/2014/09/ defense-depth-breadth-securing-internet-things/.

Sparkman, Courtney (2013, August 15). The Best Security Company: What Does it Mean? [Web log post]. Retrieved from http://www.officerreports.com/blog/the-best-security-company/.

Truman, Jennifer, L., and Lynn Langton (2015). *Criminal Victimization, 2014*, U.S. Department of Justice, Bureau of Justice Statistics. Retrieved from http://www.bjs.gov/content/pub/pdf/cv14.pdf.

Uniform Crime Reporting, https://ucr.fbi.gov/ucr.

About the Author

Salvatore "Sal" DeRose, Sr. has owned and operated Signal 88 Security of Greater Philadelphia since 2013. He is fully committed to the company's core values of passion, honesty and integrity, relationships, serving, and learning, and brings heartfelt enthusiasm to the job daily. After being honorably discharged from the U.S. Army, Sal received his B.B.A. from Temple University and his master's degree from Villanova University. He has 20+ years of experience in business, accounting, security, and information technology, and stands at the forefront of his profession. Sal belongs to a variety of industry and professional organizations and is an active member of his community, where he resides with his wife and family.

www.ingramcontent.com/pod-product-compliance
Lightning Source LLC
Chambersburg PA
CBHW050351280326
41933CB00010BA/1421
9780998359601